FIRE AT THE FREEDOM HOUSE

A Memoir from the
1966 Mississippi Civil Rights Movement

Matthew Rinaldi

Layout and design: Dave Chapple
chappledesign.com

First Edition

Published by
Audacity Press

DEDICATION

For Luther Mallett

An unsung hero of the civil rights movement

Contents

A note on language. During the time the events in this book were being experienced, the term "Negro" was considered acceptable. It appears in documents, leaflets, letters and movement press releases, which are reproduced here as originally printed for historical accuracy.

While this book was first being written, it was common to write about "black people and white people" with no letters capitalized. As this book is being published, it is grammatically correct to write of Black people and white people. I am convinced that is the correct capitalization and this final draft follows that grammatical insight.

Prologue

1954

(A recollection from the Mallett family history,
Attala County, Mississippi)

The message came to the Mallett home on a hot summer day, the kind of day you sweat so much your shirt sticks to your skin. A battered Ford sedan came rumbling up the driveway, exhaust fumes hissing from a small crack in the rusty tailpipe.

Two honks on the horn brought Charles and Lenora Mallett to the front door. The Mallets were among the hundred or so Black families who owned land in the central hills of Mississippi, a small farm where they were raising their four children. Charles didn't recognize the middle-aged Black man behind the wheel of the car, but he knew the young woman sitting next to him. His cousin, Doris.

She was crying. She could not speak. She gave Charles a hug, then burst into deep sobs as Lenora embraced her. What had happened? Her boyfriend had gone missing. He had been grabbed and taken away by a group of white men. Would Charles come help her? She couldn't stop trembling.

Charles huddled with Lenora. They knew Doris lived more than 15 miles away, on the outskirts of a small town. He could take their young sons, Luther and Wiley, with him while Lenora stayed behind with their teenage daughter, Leila Mae, and their youngest child, Jean. Somebody had to help.

Lenora fixed some tea while Charles got the pickup truck ready. Luther and Wiley climbed into the front seat with their Dad while Lenora handed Charles a thermos, kissed him and placed her hand gently on his arm. "You take good care," she whispered. He nodded.

Charles followed the Ford carrying his cousin and the driver as they journeyed north past the towns of Ethel and McCool. After that Luther and Wiley had no idea where they were or where they were going. They drove to a wooden shack, and Charles met with Doris and one of her friends. He came back to the truck grim-faced.

"We've got to head into the woods," was all he said as he climbed back into the pickup. They drove on a dirt road following the Ford until they came to a patch of ground marked by tire tracks. Charles led his sons on a trail through the forest, in the recent footsteps of many others.

Soon they had to stop. In a small clearing they saw him. The body of a young Black man hung in the forest, lifeless and still, the rope around his neck tied to a branch of a gum tree.

Charles and the other man cut the rope and lowered the young man to the ground. They wrapped him in an old blanket and carried him back to the pickup truck.

Charles was deeply unsettled. He knew the young man had been warned. Born a Black man in Mississippi, he had been warned all his life. But young and strong, he was brimming with self-confidence. Living under the rules of white supremacy in the Deep South, he had been considered uppity by some local white men. Now he had paid the price.

Luther and Wiley stood and watched. They would carry that day with them for the rest of their lives.

Introduction

Black people were a mystery to me. I was the grandson of Italian immigrants, born in Brooklyn in 1947. Oh sure, there were Black people in the world around me, but I only lived in Brooklyn until the age of three. My older sister Jane had a Black friend in elementary school, Eleanor. In one of those early childhood memories that's only a single visual image, like a snapshot, I remember seeing Eleanor sitting in the kitchen and being startled by her dark skin. I may have stared with wide-eyed wonder.

Why did she look so different?

In 1950 my parents moved us to an all-white suburb on Long Island, and Black people seemed to vanish from the world. North Valley Stream it was called, built alongside the old farming village of Valley Stream. North Valley Stream was filled with Jewish and Italian immigrants from Brooklyn. But Black people? I didn't see any in Valley Stream.

My parents bought a television sometime in the 1950s, and with the beginning of the civil rights movement I began to see Black people on the news. I saw crowds of white people, their faces contorted in anger, screaming at Black kids trying to go to high school in Little Rock, Arkansas. I saw Black college students being attacked, kicked and brutalized for sitting at lunch counters simply wanting to be served. Newspapers printed photographs of furious white men with guns mobilizing to prevent James Meredith from enrolling at Ole Miss. But these were pictures, visual images, no more personal to me than Russian soldiers or the Queen of England.

This all changed in 1963 when I was 16. In an effort to strengthen my high school record, I submitted applications to summer programs with the National Science Foundation. I was accepted for a math program at Morgan State College in Baltimore, Maryland. I had no idea that Morgan State was a historically Black college. My parents helped me pack and put me on the train to Baltimore. I took a cab from the train station to

Morgan State, and was startled to see mostly Black people. This was my first, sudden and unanticipated immersion in the Black community.

We were all high school students spending six weeks together on a college campus. A few other kids were white, but almost everyone was Black: our professor was Black, our dorm monitor was Black and my roommate, Kenneth Chestnut, was Black. If I formed any stereotype of Black teenagers in the first week, it was that Black kids are math geniuses. Our professor was hard on everyone, and while I had been seen as exceptional in high school back home, here I was at best mediocre.

What really mattered that summer was that for the first time in my life I came to know Black people as individuals. We shared an intimate life in the dorms. We met each other with our personal quirks exposed. It didn't take long to find out who had a good sense of humor, who had a positive outlook on life and who was gloomy, who was ready to flirt and maybe even kiss and who would rather hide in a corner at group events. Skin color seemed to disappear as each of our personalities emerged.

I also learned much more about racism and segregation in the South. Kids talked to me about beatings in North Carolina, rape in Louisiana and sexual abuse in Virginia, even lynchings in Georgia. I heard about the many indignities of daily life, such as always stepping aside when a white person walked toward you on the sidewalk. Most of the Black kids in the program from the South had worked with old, used textbooks in their segregated schools and had been tutored by their teachers or adult friends. All the Black kids from the South had suffered exclusion from many public places, including swimming pools, restaurants and libraries.

One seemingly small event stayed with me. As we were getting to the end of the program, my roommate, Kenneth, took me by surprise.

"Hey Matt," he said on a Saturday afternoon. "Let's go to town tonight and see Paul Newman in *Hud*."

"Why?" I responded. "I'm not so sure it's a great movie."

"Yeah, well, I'd like to find out for myself, and if I don't see it here, I may never see it."

"C'mon, why not?" I asked in disbelief.

He stared at me like I still really didn't get it.

"Because," he said with some exasperation, "the movie theater in my home town won't let people inside if they look like me." We went to see *Hud* that night.

I went back to North Valley Stream with a passion for joining the civil rights movement. This was no abstract issue anymore, no simple newspaper article. This was now about people whom I considered friends. The abuse they suffered was now personal for me. Like a young Italian boy who might be called to the priesthood, I felt called to be a civil rights activist.

Opportunities for involvement were fast in coming. The March on Washington for Jobs and Freedom was that August 28, just a few weeks after we finished our classes at Morgan State. My family went to Washington, D.C. to participate. My parents were both liberal social workers in New York, and with my sister Jane we travelled on a union-chartered train. We met one of my friends from Morgan State, Mary Diane Soloman, at the train station in D.C. We marched together and heard Martin Luther King, Jr.'s powerful "I Have a Dream" speech. It was impossible not to share that dream with him as he spoke.

Back in Valley Stream I joined Long Island CORE, the Congress of Racial Equality. Our chapter was led by a young Black man named Lincoln Lynch. I first walked a picket line at a school board meeting, protesting school segregation in the New York suburbs. I was required to participate in one training session where we were punched and kicked, perhaps too gently, to prepare us for what we might encounter during non-violent protests. We worked against job discrimination in the North and against housing segregation on Long Island. We went door to door to register voters in the predominantly Black town of Hempstead, and for one afternoon we were joined by Martin Luther King, Jr., who radiated confidence that we could change the world.

In 1964 I was still in high school and too young to go to Mississippi's Freedom Summer, but we raised money and collected books to send to the Freedom Schools.

My path was set when Lincoln Lynch brought a CORE staff member who worked in Mississippi to a meeting on Long Island. This young white man wore the trademark denim overalls of a civil rights field organizer and was seeking recruits for organizing projects in Mississippi. He seemed like the bravest person I had ever met. I wanted to be him.

My college "strategy" worked and I was admitted to Oberlin College, which I knew had a history of students participating in the Southern civil rights movement. For me, going South was the mark of true commitment. With a mixture of youthful enthusiasm, male bravado, the adolescent myth of invincibility and the desire to make a difference, I was ready to head to Mississippi.

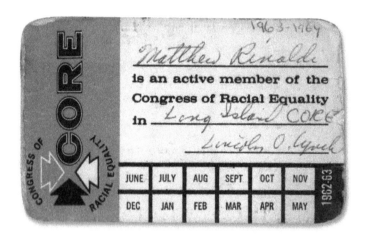

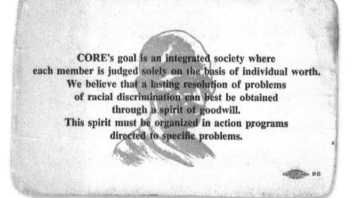

Chapter 1:
Welcome to Mississippi

We left for Mississippi late on a Saturday afternoon in January of 1966. Travelling in five cars, we were a group of 24 mostly white students from Oberlin College in Ohio. We had been recruited to spend our winter break working with the Mississippi Freedom Democratic Party (MFDP). A few of the older students were veterans of the movement, but many of us were freshmen entering the Deep South for the first time. We were idealistic, adventurous and woefully inexperienced.

I was in the first car to leave campus. None of the women on the trip were in our car. We were five adolescent guys in an era of no seatbelts, young enough to sleep in awkward positions in the back seat until it was our turn to drive. One of us always sat in the front to keep the driver awake. The direction was southwest, but there was no direct route, so we drove 600 miles in the dark from Oberlin to Columbus to Louisville to Memphis, each of us taking turns driving and sleeping.

The other guys in the car were not people I knew well. We talked about school and classes and girls, about our backgrounds, mostly about our families or where we grew up. What we didn't talk about was our feelings, our mounting anxiety and fear about the journey we were on.

We reached Memphis, near the Tennessee-Mississippi border, sometime in the transition from darkness to dawn. Dick Klausner took over the driving. He was older and had already been to the Deep South twice. Klausner was a short, stocky guy from Iowa with a head of bushy dark hair, and most of us thought he was the toughest guy in the group. He was built like a wrestler and spoke with an easy confidence. Klausner began driving just before we entered Mississippi.

His first precaution was to fill the car with gas before we crossed the state line. He pulled into a highway gas station with a small convenience store. We all needed something to eat. We had packed plenty of warm clothes and sleeping bags, since it was winter in Ohio, but we had neglected to bring much food. I climbed out of the car, stretched, breathed in the sharp morning air and headed inside for snacks and coffee.

The white gas station attendant seemed to know exactly what we were about. Maybe he really did, maybe there was something about our awkwardness that revealed our intentions to him. When he had finished pumping the gas and we were back in the car, he leaned in with a big grin and gave us the traditional Southern farewell, "Y'all come back!" His grin made me uneasy.

His words put me in touch with the reality that we might not come back. I kept thinking about Andrew Goodman, the New York college student who had been killed within 36 hours of entering Mississippi. He went missing with civil rights workers James Chaney and Michael Schwerner at the beginning of Freedom Summer in 1964. Chaney was a Black Mississippian who knew his life was always at risk. Schwerner was a white New Yorker who had been in the state long enough to be well known to the Klan. All three were abducted in Neshoba County on June 21 in 1964, taken to a deserted country road and murdered. Their bodies were not found until early August. Andy Goodman barely had time to look around. Most of us in the car were just like him, newcomers hurtling toward trouble.

Klausner hit the road, and it was no comfort when we crossed the border and passed the state flag and a huge billboard decorated with magnolias and the words "Welcome to Mississippi." The flag of Mississippi, which I looked at closely for the first time, carried a message. The upper left quadrant contained the battle flag of the Confederacy. In my mind, the message was "Welcome to the Land of Slavery." Someone in the car quipped, "Hey Yankees, welcome back to the Civil War."

We started out on the long drive down Highway 51. From the car window I watched the sun rising over forests and farmland stretching from the roadside to the horizon. There seemed to be water everywhere. Creeks and streams ran alongside the road, ponds appeared every few miles. Just north of Batesville we crossed the Tallahatchie River, its waters rushing toward the Mississippi River. Where the land was undisturbed, we passed small herds of deer grazing in the early morning sun, hawks circling above and egrets posing motionless in shallow water, watchful of the chance to spear a fish for breakfast.

We were traveling on the eastern edge of the Delta, that broad flat land of rich soil from the alluvial plain of the Mississippi River, pungent and fertile, home of vast cotton plantations, the infamous Parchman prison and the birthplace of the Delta blues. Isolated farmhouses were spread among expanses of fields waiting for summer crops. Much of the land was filled with stands of oak, barren of leaves in the grey winter, though the pine trees still held their needles. We slowed down to pass through the towns of Hernando, Batesville and Grenada.

Klausner knew the radio stations, and as the day brightened on rural shacks we listened to the blues as only a Southern Black radio station in the sixties could play them, with Black disc jockeys, few commercials and lots of music, guitar pickers, pianos and horns and harmonicas, trembling bass and voices pained and seductive.

As we drove south we listened to old-time singers like Bessie Smith, recordings by Mississippi John Hurt and new sounds like B.B. King and Motown. The music filled the car as we watched people in the small towns start their Sunday - poor Blacks rising from wooden shacks that looked ready to collapse, poor whites not much better off, walking down the road or driving beaten-up old cars, all looking like they were dressed for church. Klausner kept the wheel for over 200 miles until we reached Jackson and the MFDP office on North Farish Street.

The winter before, while I was still in high school, students from Oberlin had gone to Mississippi to help rebuild a church burned to the ground after a rally led by Fannie Lou Hamer. The project was called Carpenters for Christmas, and the frame of the church was rebuilt in time for Christmas services. This year we were being asked by the MFDP to be field organizers, direct participants in the fight against white supremacy.

The MFDP had been birthed during the organizing for Freedom Summer in 1964, when almost a thousand Northern students had gone to Mississippi to register Black voters and establish Freedom Schools. By 1966 the MFDP was the most significant civil rights organization in the state. Led by Lawrence Guyot, Fannie Lou Hamer, Annie Devine and a network of local activists, the MFDP still welcomed the participation of white Northerners. It was a natural fit for Oberlin students.

We spent more than a few hours in Jackson. While we waited to see where they would send us we gathered up our parental consent forms. I was a freshman, 18 years old, and the MFDP wanted everyone under 21 to have the written consent of a parent or guardian. The forms were to protect the movement from criminal charges of contributing to the delinquency of a minor, so I had brought one home during Christmas break to get my parents to sign.

We had talked about it sitting at the small kitchen table in Valley Stream. My parents were both opposed to racial prejudice and believed in working to heal the world. They were also protective of me and very worried about my safety. This was not easy for them.

"You know we support your ideals," my father said, "but do you want to die?"

"No, of course not. But most civil rights workers who go South don't die." This was true, but many were beaten, and I was secretly terrified of being beaten. I kept that to myself.

"Oh my god," my mother exclaimed. "I saw the mothers crying at the funeral after those kids were found buried in Mississippi. You want me in the newspapers crying my eyes out?"

"Not at all. I'm not doing this to hurt you. I'm doing this because I want to make a difference," was the best I could muster at first. Maybe I also craved adventure and felt drawn by the lure of danger, but I rarely admitted that, even to myself. I got up from the table and paced in the kitchen, trying to think of what to say. Finally I added, "And where do you see Italian kids in Mississippi? We should be a part of this movement."

This hit their weak spot. Both of my parents were ashamed of what they saw as the rough character of Italian-Americans in New York. As young people they had separately vowed not to marry an Italian, and in that way they were perfect for each other when they met in social work school. They both believed in the civil rights movement and, alongside their fear, they were quietly proud of my involvement. I got their signatures.

We continued to wait in the Farish Street office in Jackson after we handed in our forms. The MFDP was taking part in a Poor People's Conference at Mount Beulah near the town of Edwards. Mount Beulah had been a Black college and was now the headquarters of the Delta Ministry, a mainstay of the movement. That winter hundreds of Black farm workers and cotton pickers in the Delta had organized the Freedom Labor Union and had tried to strike for higher wages. Many were paid as little as three dollars a day. The strike had little impact, and many strikers were fired from their jobs and thrown off the plantations. Now they were homeless and camped out in tents in a makeshift Strike City. The conference was searching for a plan to deal with this crisis. The Jackson office was a flurry of activity.

While we waited a group of us went to eat at the E&L Barbeque, about a mile away on Bailey Avenue. Slow-cooked meat, ribs and tips and chunks of chicken and pork, slathered with sauce after hitting the heat, smoky food we could smell from two blocks away, this was my first experience of Southern cooking. Growing up I had eaten great Italian food made by my grandmothers in Brooklyn, but I had never had food with a kick. I learned in Mississippi that grilling hotdogs and hamburgers over charcoal briquettes in the backyard in Valley Stream simply was not barbeque.

I also learned in Jackson that day that there could be substantial meals for a northern civil rights worker with money. We ate well. The cash in our pockets was a resource that most local activists and civil rights workers lacked.

We returned to the office, where this contrast became sharp. The pressing need being discussed at the Poor People's Conference was feeding the plantation workers at Strike City. The people who were camping out were hungry. The federal government had sent thousands of pounds of surplus food, known as "commodities," to Mississippi, but distribution was being held up at the state level.

It was also historically cold that winter in Mississippi. We had expected the South to be warmer than Ohio, but one night that January was the coldest on record in Mississippi, with the temperature close to zero. The plantation workers who were camping at Strike City were freezing.

There was talk that hundreds of people might move into abandoned portions of the Greenville Air Force Base. The first group had already camped near the base. Unita Blackwell, born to plantation workers in the Delta town of Lula, Mississippi and now an MFDP leader in Issaquena County, was a driving force behind this plan. There simply was no time to focus on our group from Oberlin.

It was finally decided that all of us should go to Edwards for the night. We could join the end of the Poor People's Conference in Mount Beulah and find a place to sleep in the old college dormitories. In the early evening we finally headed west, in the direction of Vicksburg and the Mississippi River. Klausner was still driving.

We arrived at Mount Beulah near the end of the mass meeting. We could hear the sound of singing coming from a large auditorium. Someone brought us inside. Music filled a massive hall packed with people, mostly Black but with a sprinkling of whites, all joined in song.

The singing may have been led by members of the Freedom Singers from SNCC, the Student Nonviolent Coordinating Committee, or by voices from local gospel choirs. The first song I heard spoke directly to the plight of the Black plantation workers:

> *I'm gonna sit at the welcome table*
> *Oh Lordy*
> *I'm gonna sit at the welcome table one of these days*
> *Hallelujah!*
> *I'm gonna sit at the welcome table*
> *Gonna sit at the welcome table*
> *One of these days.*
>
> *All God's children gonna sit together*
> *Oh Lordy*
> *All God's children gonna sit together one of these days*
> *Hallelujah!*
> *All God's children gonna sit together*
> *Gonna sit together at the table*
> *One of these days.*

Most of the people in the auditorium came from communities that often joined together in song, particularly in church services. Their voices had grown strong with gospel and blues. Now we were singing songs to push away the fear, to unite people, to express in one voice a feeling that was pained and wounded and scared and determined.

It has been said by veterans of the civil rights movement that the movement itself was a form of musical. We had a song for everything. We could adapt a song to the moment. If we were about to be clubbed by Sheriff Williams, we'd sing "Ain't Gonna Let Sheriff Williams Turn Me Around." Every action was set to song, usually by Black civil rights workers who had grown up in the South, who not only sang at church but also sang and danced at juke joints and for whom the music of the civil rights movement was part of a culture filled with song. For Northern white civil rights workers, for me, the experience of being in the Deep South was steeped in music.

The next song was directed at the white Governor of Mississippi, "Ain't Gonna Let Paul Johnson Turn Me 'Round." It was followed by the favorite of Fannie Lou Hamer, "This Little Light of Mine." We were there in time to join hands with total strangers and sway with the music, to be carried away with our shared voices and commitment, singing the closing song for all mass meetings, "We Shall Overcome." I fought back the tears welling in my eyes. Welcome to Mississippi, welcome to the struggle in the Deep South. We embrace you.

As the meeting broke up I waited around for someone to tell me what to do next. Dick Klausner was asked to drive a back-up car escorting Fannie Lou Hamer to the home where she was staying. Somehow I was picked to ride with him. I wound up in the front seat of a Buick with Klausner driving as we followed the car carrying Mrs. Hamer. Its taillights glowed red ahead of us in the darkness of the country road.

Klausner told me to watch for headlights behind us, in case night riders had been waiting for the meeting to end so they could do harm to Mrs. Hamer. I turned around in my seat in order to look out the rear window. The road passed through a stretch of sweeping curves and low rolling hills, and I watched behind us for the first glow of headlights, to see if someone was following us. Just as I was beginning to relax, the road behind us lit up.

"Someone's behind us," I said, sudden alarm in my voice. I felt a tightening in my body, my muscles clenching from my throat to the pit of my stomach. Klausner accelerated immediately, blinking his high beams to alert the car ahead of us carrying Mrs. Hamer. They sped up and together we raced along the road.

"Are they still following us?" he asked.

At the crest of the next hill I could still see the glow of light through the back window. They were still behind us. I managed only a grunt that meant we were still being followed.

"What do you see now?' Klausner asked moments later, seeming calm as he continued to press on the gas pedal.

By the turn of the next curve the road and night sky behind us was dark.

"I think they're gone," I told him. We had left them behind, and they didn't seem to be speeding to catch up with us. Klausner waited a minute before he blinked his high beams again and began to slow down. We followed the car in front of us as it turned left off the main road. Mrs. Hamer had arrived safely. We drove back to Mt. Beulah mostly in silence, listening to the quiet and still watching for headlights. I tried to calm myself down. This was my first experience of sustained fear, a feeling which was to remain my shadow companion every day in Mississippi.

We returned to the dormitories and were given a place to sleep. I had a warm sleeping bag and huddled inside as I hugged the pillow on the narrow bed. My mind was racing from the events of the day until I finally managed to fall asleep.

The next morning the biting cold air woke me up. We shared a communal breakfast of powdered eggs, grits, biscuits and coffee with everyone being housed by the Delta Ministry. Word quickly spread that seven carloads of conference participants, led by Unita Blackwell, were already heading for the abandoned portion of Greenville Air Force Base. They had made it onto the base itself and were soon joined by over a hundred people from the tents of Strike City.

After we ate and packed up, it was time to move on. A few Oberlin students stayed behind to help with a leaflet and mailing in support of the occupation. The plantation workers were intent on staying in the empty barracks until their demands were met. The most immediate need was the distribution of the federal food commodities. The leaflet proclaimed, "We are here because we are hungry and cold and have no jobs or land. We don't want charity. We are willing to work for ourselves if given a chance."

The rest of us returned to Jackson. While we waited the group from Mt. Beulah caught up with us. The MFDP leadership stayed with the plan to send us out to organizing projects. One car with four students went to Natchez to work with Charles Evers, including Glanetta Miller and Penny Zolbrod, Black and white roommates at Oberlin. One car went to Canton. The rest of us were sent to support the MFDP effort in the city of

Fire at the Freedom House

Kosciusko in Attala County. This was new territory even for the veterans in our group. We took off within a few minutes of receiving our assignment, venturing into the unknown.

The Freedom House in Kosciusko.
Photo by Matthew Rinaldi

Chapter 2:
Cold Mud in Kosciusko

We left Jackson on a paved highway, heading north toward the rolling hills of central Mississippi. We had spent our first two days on the southern edge of the Delta. Now the landscape became open fields and farmland, set amidst forests of pine and cypress trees dripping with Spanish moss.

This land had once been Choctaw territory. The Choctaw people and the Chickasaw to the north had survived a Spanish attack by Hernando de Soto's expedition in 1541 and centuries of incursions by the French travelling the waterways from Louisiana before finally being pushed out by Anglo settlers from Alabama and Georgia in the 1830s. Those settlers brought with them enslaved African people. What we saw now as we entered Attala County and crossed the Yockanookany River was a world of poor farmers, Black and Anglo, eking out a living from the soil. It had been a rainy winter and the river swirled with dark cloudy water as it churned its way south.

We were headed to the Freedom House in Kosciusko. In the movement at that time any house could be a Freedom House. It was the name given to whatever structure was used as a movement center by organizers living and working in a community. The map given to us by an MFDP organizer in Jackson took us off the asphalt and led to a network of dirt roads. There had been rain in the afternoon and the roads were filled with puddles. We followed tracks of tire tread in the cold mud.

We arrived in a slight drizzle, with at least two dozen Black people waiting for us in front of a dilapidated shack with a painted sign nailed above the front window proclaiming it to be a Freedom House. I remember pulling up and being greeted with great excitement. Some of the kids ran to the neighbors shouting, "The freedom riders are here, the freedom riders are here." By 1966 the term "freedom riders" was often used to describe all civil rights workers in Mississippi, not just people who were part of the original Freedom Rides into Jackson in 1961.

I needed to ease slowly into this reality. It was not totally unfamiliar. Like most white Northerners in the sixties, I had seen photographs of poor rural communities in the Deep South in the newspapers. Here I was in that world, surrounded by wooden houses set together in a small community. Most homes looked like sharecroppers' shacks, but they weren't standing alone on isolated farmland. Instead they were clustered together like a small village. I looked at the shacks and the trees and the grey skies. As I looked at the people who had been waiting for us, I took a deep breath, lowered my emotional defenses and got ready to meet many new people.

A large group of Black teenagers and a few younger kids greeted us, and they were the source of the excitement and commotion. Some adults stood gathered in small groups. Luther Mallett was there with the high school students, but we didn't meet that day. Once I walked into this setting and began mingling with people, I was introduced to Pearl and Edgar Nash, who had a house across the dirt road from the Freedom House.

Mr. Nash was in his sixties, neatly groomed and a bit on the quiet side. Mrs. Nash was his exact opposite and perfect complement, with lots of energy and plenty to say. She was effusive in welcoming us. "Son," she said to me, "anytime you need anything, you just walk on over and knock." She smiled and added, "Don't you mind if Mr. Nash doesn't say much. He's just about deaf."

Two more cars arrived, also packed with students from Oberlin. By the time we had all arrived there were 18 of us, and we all needed places to stay. We also needed a way to keep in touch, some communication system and some way to figure out how to set up transportation. Fortunately for us there was a network of people working together as the local MFDP. They had already figured who would house students and how many. I have no idea how they made their plans, but everything seemed to get sorted out with relative ease. Many of the people there greeting us were ready to take home some of these Northern "freedom riders."

Amidst the crowd one figure stood out, a very tall thin white man. He was wearing a warm dark shirt and dungarees that looked like they were about to fall off his hips. He had dark hair and a scraggly short beard. He was so much taller than anyone else that my eyes were immediately drawn

Fire at the Freedom House

to him. This was Gunter Frentz, the contact person whose name had been given to us by the Jackson office. His expression was that of someone who had just received a wonderful present. At some point, while we were still gathered outside as a group, Gunter raised his arms above his head and got people's attention.

"Listen up," he said. He told us that a group of armed white men had confronted him at the Freedom House the night before and that shots were fired. "These men are armed and I don't know when they might come back. We plan to defend ourselves. We are all in danger and we need people with some experience with guns to stay at the Freedom House." He probably addressed this to the guys, though I doubt he would have declined a female student who stepped forward.

It is impossible for me to know how each person reacted to these words. Most of us were taken by surprise. The civil rights movement was known to the nation as a nonviolent movement. Wasn't that what Rev. King was preaching? Wasn't that why we saw young people on TV getting food and garbage dumped on their heads at lunch counter sit-ins without reacting? Wasn't that why people curled themselves into the fetal position while they were being kicked and beaten? We had driven almost a thousand miles to participate in the Southern civil rights movement. The idea that we would be handed guns upon arrival in Kosciusko was beyond comprehension.

Some of us were not shocked. A few of the civil rights veterans in our group knew that there had always been some level of self-defense practiced by Black communities in the Deep South, and the arrival of the movement had not caused Black people to disarm. My only experience to that point had been with Long Island CORE, which practiced nonviolence, but I was an insatiable reader and I knew things were different in the South. I knew that during one of the trainings for Freedom Summer in 1964, Bob Moses had talked about guns and had said to the volunteers, "If you were in a house which was under attack, and the owner was shot, and there were kids there, and you could take his gun to protect them – should you? I can't answer that. I don't think anyone can answer that." [1] Northern civil rights workers had written in *Letters From Mississippi*, a collection of letters from Freedom Summer volunteers, that local families who had housed them had posted armed guards, family members and friends, outside their homes.[2]

I knew that just three weeks earlier, on January 10, NAACP leader Vernon Dahmer and his family had been attacked by night riders in Hattiesburg, Mississippi. Their home had been firebombed and set ablaze. As his wife and children fled, Mr. Dahmer had fired back at the attackers from the burning house long enough for his family to escape. He died in the hospital the next day from smoke inhalation. I also knew we were standing less than 40 miles from the spot on Rock Cut Road in Neshoba County where Goodman, Chaney and Schwerner had been murdered. We were not in a safe area. Some books about the Deep South had photographs of armed Black men guarding homes and churches, so I was not completely surprised, in January of 1966, to be offered a gun by the civil rights movement.

I'd had some training with a rifle. The summer after Morgan State I had gone to another National Science Foundation high school program, this one at Mount Hermon School in Massachusetts. It had a mandatory physical education requirement, and one option was rifle range. Training was exclusively on a .22 caliber rifle. I earned certificates as a marksman and a sharpshooter. Since the movement in Attala County was already practicing armed self-defense, in my opinion it was not only ethical but almost imperative to participate with the Black community in sharing this risk.

At the same time, what Gunter said was alarming. If there had been an attack the night before, when would they come back? I volunteered to be a guard at the Freedom House mostly because it felt like the right choice. But there was another reason I stepped forward. I volunteered because I was quite afraid of being kicked and beaten, and I felt safer with the chance to defend myself. At least one other Oberlin student, James Hudock, stepped forward without hesitation. I think he had been around guns and had gone hunting with his dad. Ultimately, six of us, all guys, including Dick Klausner and Don Salisbury, stayed at the Freedom House with Gunter.

The other Oberlin students went home that night with the adults who had gathered to greet us or with kids sent to bring them home to their families. One car stayed at the Freedom House, but we had two other cars that were used to move students and their stuff - sleeping bags and clothes and sundries - to the homes where they were staying. Some people walked to homes close by, following paths through the woods.

I settled in, stretching my borrowed sleeping bag out on one of the cots in the front room. I didn't have a gun yet, but I expected someone to hand me one before it got dark. Where did the guns come from? The local community armed us. It was not unusual for a Southern family to have several guns. Most households owned a rifle or a shotgun, in the Black community as well as the white, and it was not uncommon for women to have access to a handgun. We were provided with an eclectic mix - a small collection of pistols, rifles and shotguns, none of them high-tech weapons, even by the standards of the day. We had one pump shotgun, which could fire up to five shells. All the rest were either single-shot rifles or double-barreled shotguns, which meant you had to crack open the gun to insert two cardboard shells side by side, one in each barrel. I was comfortable when Gunter handed me a single-shot .22 rifle. It was the weapon I had been trained on and the only type of gun I had ever fired. It felt familiar in my hands.

We divided shifts of time for guard duty so at least two people were up and alert at all times during the night. The house had three rooms set in a straight row front to back, a type often called a shotgun shack. The back room was occupied by Gunter. The six of us from Oberlin were assigned to sleep in the front and middle rooms. By unrolling my sleeping bag I had claimed a cot in the front room, which also had a gas heater. Being in a room with a heater was a blessing. It also may have been dangerous, since the building itself was flimsy and the heat was generated by open flames from a row of small burners mounted on a gas line backed by a metal sheet. The metal reflected the heat back into the room. The people on watch for night riders could also watch for any sudden fire from the gas flames. I was exhausted and fell asleep quickly, the .22 rifle within easy reach underneath the cot.

I was awakened in the middle of the night for a turn at guard duty. I pulled myself out of the sleeping bag, the cold air biting my lungs, put on my shoes and took hold of the rifle. Being on guard duty required staying alert and watching the street and the side yard. There were no people out walking that late at night. Three or four times one of us went outside. I went out for long stretches and walked among the trees on the hillside next to the Freedom House, looking for any sign of human activity. At one point a beaten-up Chevy came slowly down the road. I took partial cover behind an oak tree, and the lone Black man driving the car waved to me. It remained very quiet and brutally cold. After a few hours we woke up the next shift and I dropped off to sleep again.

In the morning we took turns going across the street to the home of Pearl and Edgar Nash. They were both retired Black teachers who taught in the Black segregated schools. They lived in a one-story house with running water and electricity, a large kitchen, comfortable furniture and a large bathroom. They were incredibly generous and let those of us staying at the Freedom House use their bathroom and shower every morning. A few times that week Mrs. Nash told us that she had made breakfast and invited us to sit down and eat, usually eggs and grits and bacon, or fried slices of some salty meat, and coffee. A real feast.

Other mornings we bought breakfast at Izah Brown's small grocery and kitchen. He lived a short walk from the Freedom House and ran a small business out of his house. There were a few round tables and chairs in a room that might once have been the living room. He had transformed the room into a store, with snacks and sundries for sale. The room also had a counter that opened into his kitchen, and in the morning he served breakfast. Mr. Brown was a strong supporter of the civil rights movement and was happy to see us in his store. Some afternoons we might walk over to his place and indulge in soda and thick sticky buns that came wrapped in plastic bags.

Every day we did voter registration work. Gunter and Betty Jones, his organizing partner who was home that week in Vicksburg, had mapped out the Black community within the Kosciusko city limits and the areas that needed to be canvassed. Our task was to go out in small groups and let people know that they could register. Federal law had been changing quickly, and rules which for years had been used to prevent Black people from voting were being eliminated.

The poll tax in federal elections was banned in 1964 by the 24th Amendment to the U.S. Constitution. The Voting Rights Act of 1965 prohibited the literacy test in federal and state elections. The U.S. Supreme Court would ban the poll tax in state elections within weeks, on March

24, with its ruling in *Harper v. Virginia Board of Elections*, 383 U.S. 663 (1966). Our task was made easier because of the victories of those who had been active before us.

The veterans in our group gave us some direction. Martha Honey, who had been an organizer in Holmes County, had solid advice. "People may be very wary when you knock on the door. It will be clear to them who we are - civil rights workers on the porch. Some people will welcome us, or at least be curious about us. But for many Black people this can be very threatening. They will suddenly have white people on the porch. When is this good news for a Black person in Mississippi?"

Another veteran urged us not to rush people. "You have no business pushing them to do something they're not ready to do. They'll be polite, but a lot of people will tell you what they think you want to hear. That doesn't mean they're ready to register."

Someone recounted a story about a play put on by some youngsters at a Freedom School. "So this young girl plays the part of an older man faced with a persistent civil rights worker named Earl. 'Yes sir, Mister Earl, I'll be going down to register tomorrow, that's for sure.' And this goes on week after week, but the man never registers. Finally Earl gives up and the man breathes a sigh of relief."

We knew we were outsiders in someone else's community for just a brief time in the middle of the winter. At least we were working under the direction of the Mississippi Freedom Democratic Party. The best role we could fill was to follow their direction and work on the tasks they felt were the most important.

We were given stacks of Applications for Registration and sent out into the community. I went out with the group that was staying at the Freedom House, with Gunter driving. We went to some shacks in the countryside, still within the city limits. Most were wooden, though a few were covered with textured tar paper that made them look like they were brick. All had some form of covered front porch, making it easy to knock on the door and wait. Gunter let us practice. "Introduce yourself. Make eye contact. Be patient. Most important, be deferential. You'll be meeting people who've been forced to be deferential to white folks all their lives."

Traveling with Gunter made everything easier. Many people already knew him. Almost everyone had heard of him, the tall thin white northerner who had come to town with a Black woman from Vicksburg, Betty Jones. A few were bold about it. "You that Gunner fella?"

We took turns starting the conversation. Gunter would let us go on awhile, maybe to see how we'd do, but he was quick to interrupt and take over. There were people who were not eager to see us and seemed either suspicious or afraid of being seen with us on their porch. A few would take the application, promise to register, and quickly close the door. We were careful not to push people.

In many cases, the person at the door would finish looking us over within a few minutes and would say, "Well, don't just stand out there in the cold. Come on in and have a sit." Most living rooms were small and a bit tattered but furnished with some comfortable "sink into me" furniture. Being invited in with Gunter made it easy for me and the other students to be more passive. He had no hesitation when starting a conversation. He would listen as well as talk, but we were observers. People who invited us in were extremely gracious and generous, offering us something to drink, usually water or tea, and often something to eat. Some people were already registered to vote and were supporters of the MFDP, but still they were curious about the group of students who had arrived in town and they wanted to be brought up to date.

I learned that there was more than fear preventing some people from registering. Although the laws were changing, the behavior of white Southerners in charge of registering voters was not always changing along with the law. I made a note at the time concerning Mr. DeWitt Thurmon, 72 years old, a man who had been born in Mississippi and lived here all his life. The note read, "Went down before Christmas. Told registrar that he couldn't read. Registrar said that he couldn't vote." This was long after the literacy requirement had been outlawed in federal and state elections.

A phone call to the office of the Center for Civil Rights Under Law brought us a visit the very next day from Ollie Rosenbaum, a white lawyer working from Jackson. He met with the white City Attorney, Aaron Condon, who had a conversation with the white voter registrar. The law had changed, the white community knew it, and Aaron Condon was an unusually fair-minded attorney.

Mr. Thurmon was allowed to register.

Chapter 3:
The Intimacy of Sitting Together

With the active encouragement of the local MFDP supporters, we did far more than voter registration. We took on segregation in the local restaurants. As we had sung at Mt. Beulah, "All gonna sit together at the table one of these days."

The system of physical separation of white people and Black people in the Deep South extended to any situation where people might sit down together. There is an intimacy in sitting together. It puts people close together in a way that is relaxed, one that may even involve touching. It puts people on a more equal level. Sitting together violates the visceral rules of racial separation. This was true in all public aspects of social interaction between whites and Blacks.

Standing together was acceptable. Stores on the courthouse square, like Boyd's Drug Store or the Merchants and Farmers Bank, welcomed Black customers, because everyone stood. There were white boys in town who went to watch football games at the Black high school, Tipton High, but who stood rather than sit with Black people. Sitting together, in the football stands or on a bus or in a café, was taboo.

In the first few days we sat with local Blacks in integrated groups in cafés, restaurants and eating places in Kosciusko like the B&F Grill and the Tuk-A-Way Diner. These were traditional sit-ins. We were not armed. The fact that we had no training as a group in nonviolent direct action didn't seem to matter.

We fully expected to have food poured on our heads or thrown in our faces or to be pulled from our seats and beaten on the floor, as we had seen so often on TV or read about in the newspapers. The first restaurant sit-in was near the courthouse square. Many of the northern whites, perhaps six or seven of us, were joined by at least that many local Black high school students. They were a pretty impressive group. Appearing calm and determined, they stood in small clusters, a few of them talking with Gunter. They were better dressed than those of us from Oberlin, with their ironed skirts and blouses, clean slacks and sweaters or jackets, while we wore rumpled clothes and bulky winter coats. There were a few conversations between local students and a few of us from the North, but I felt folded up within myself and worried.

I knew nothing about the planning, which must have been happening in the group around Gunter. I had no idea how we would enter the restaurant or where we would sit or how we would behave, but I trusted the folks who were figuring it out and in turn I felt completely accepted by all of them. Still, I felt uneasy with their acceptance, since I'd never been in a similar situation before and I didn't really know if I could handle it. Temperament could be a huge factor in these situations, and at that age I had no idea how I would respond if I was attacked or how my testosterone, adrenaline and personality would mix. At least there was strength in the size of our group, so many of us that I felt some comfort. I would have been really scared if there had been only four of us, which had been the case for the first students to sit in at the Woolworths counter in North Carolina in 1960. I didn't know how the local Chief of Police, Herbert A. Harvey, would react, parked in a police car with a deputy across the street.

Before we entered the restaurant I was one of a group assigned to sit at the counter. Most of the students were sitting at the tables, all of us in integrated groups. There was a husky local guy sitting on my right. There was an Oberlin student on my left. The person who made the most lasting impression was the white waitress, solidly built and scowling. A woman with prominent dark eyebrows, her face held a combination of contempt and amusement. She took her pencil and her order pad and put them down on the counter.

Looking stern, she said to me, "We don't serve nigger-lovers here."

I knew this line. By this time I had read more than a few descriptions of sit-in encounters, and I knew that the standard hostile opening line was "We don't serve niggers here." Perhaps by this time the line was also part of Southern folklore, for this white woman in Kosciusko seemed to know the line as well and had come up with her own variation when confronted by a white Northerner at her counter.

I did my best to duel with her. "I don't want to order a nigger-lover," I said as I tried to parry her variation of the opening line. I looked at the sign that read R.C. Cola – 5 Cents. "I want a cola."

She looked me over. "We'll see what you get." She made a notation on her order pad and moved on.

This dialog, or some variation of it, was going on throughout the restaurant. Two white waitresses were dealing with us, and they were pressed to the limit. I looked around the place and did not see any trouble brewing. There were no clusters of white people gathering outside. There were no groups of angry young white men looking at us with menace in their hearts. We were not about to be assaulted. Instead, two white customers at a table looked at us in amazement, surprised that this event had arrived out of nowhere in their small town.

We waited and waited for service, but I felt safe and mildly triumphant. When our food arrived, in my case a half a glass of ice with a small amount of cola splashed in, I didn't know enough about restaurants to worry about what else might have been in the glass. I was happy just to be served. I drank the cola. We soon had checks, everything overpriced, something like $1.40 for my cola, but those of us from Oberlin had money and paid all the bills. Money was not the issue. We had been served and we had survived. Sweet victory.

We left in an organized way, one small group at a time. When we were outside on the sidewalk everyone was relieved and glowing, but this was not the time or place to hold any kind of celebration. We shared our joy briefly, groups of people leaving in different directions. None of us noticed another car, parked further down the block. Four white men sat in that car, watching us quietly.

In the next few days, integrated groups entered every public restaurant and café in the city of Kosciusko. This wasn't as difficult as it might seem, since there were at most five or six places to eat. In every one we eventually got served, and we went back to a few places more than once during that week. We never actually got much to eat, but we helped open up the eateries to the Black community from that time forward.

In addition to the restaurants, we took on another taboo. We made an effort to integrate the Kosciusko movie theater.

White supremacy at a movie house which allowed Black patrons was difficult for me to understand at first.

The prohibition on sitting together becomes charged with sexuality when it involves sitting together in the dark. The suggestion of intimacy was particularly electric in movie theaters, where it was not uncommon, North or South, for the darkness of a movie theater to be an opportunity for couples to hold hands and touch, even kiss. Physical separation of whites and Blacks in movie theaters was mandatory in the old South.

In Kosciusko we were confronted with the Strand, the only movie theater in Attala County. The Strand sold tickets to everyone at the same price, but it enforced its own form of segregation. There was no way white people would be forced to sit with Black people. The solution? White people got the entire downstairs. Black people could only sit in the balcony.

The Strand was located on Madison Street, half a block from the town square. Painted lime green, it made a striking impression. It had one ticket window but two entrances. The double doors on the left of the ticket window led to the main floor. The single door on the right led to the balcony. Though the doors were not marked or labeled in any way, like so many aspects of segregation, especially in small towns, it was simply "known" that the downstairs was whites only and the balcony was for Black people. The Black high school students, who were the driving force in our efforts to integrate businesses in Kosciusko, were passionate about integrating the Strand. "I pay the same good money as the white kids. I want to see the movie the same way."

We were organized into small integrated groups and drove over to the town square. It was winter, and even though we were going to the early show, the 7:20 p.m. showing of *Ship of Fools*, it was already dark. The square itself had plenty of parking, making it an easy walk to the movie theater. We attracted some stares from people, but there was nothing obvious about what we were about to do. It was easy enough to go up to the ticket counter and buy a ticket. It wasn't until some of the Black teenagers went through the main doors that our intent became obvious. The usher was so taken by surprise that a large number of us got inside before the management took action. At that point the doors were suddenly closed. I hadn't made it inside in time, so this was one action I missed.

Instead I stood in the cold on Madison Street until our group decided to drive home. I was dropped off at the Freedom House with two other Oberlin students.

Later that evening I heard from those who got seats together inside the Strand. Tension was high, but at first no one created a disturbance and management decided to start the movie. As our integrated groups sat in their seats, they started being hit by candy and food thrown at them by white teenagers. Two Kosciusko police officers arrived at the theater after a quick call from management. The movie was stopped and the lights came on. One of the officers walked up and down the aisles, not saying a word. The throwing stopped. The lights were dimmed and the movie resumed. This happened at least twice before the crowd was silenced.

A copy of the police report of that night recounts the statement of one local white youngster who was in the Strand. In his words, "he sat behind the civil rights group and is aware that they were pelted with eggs and ice shavings but he denied throwing anything. He said the boy that sat next to him threw some eggs but he refused to identify this boy or anyone else in the theater that night. He said that he did not intend to 'squeal' on anyone."

The report also contains the confession of one white male teenager. He admitted he was at the Strand that night when "it was integrated by a racially mixed group of civil rights workers. He said he sat behind the group and during the movie he threw one egg and some shaved ice at the white civil rights worker known as 'fuzzy chin', name unknown. He said he knew other eggs and shaved ice were thrown but he does not know who threw them. He added the Kosciusko Police Department was present and when the officers were in the theater the throwing would stop but when they left the throwing would start again."

To the credit of the management of the Strand, the film was shown to its conclusion in the darkened, integrated theater.

Attala County had been stirred up more than we could have imagined in just a few days. All our efforts had gone so smoothly that it was easy to become relaxed. Some white people seemed ready to accept what looked like an inevitable new reality. We were soon to learn that within the white community there was another, older, more intransigent point of view. A maroon Plymouth arrived at the Strand after the police were called. It parked in the town square. In the car were two white men, just watching.

Mississippi map and surrounding area

Chapter 4:
Squeeze It

The next morning the Black high school students had to be back in school at Tipton High. Most of the Oberlin students got the chance to sleep in. Everyone had stayed up late, fueled by adrenaline from the events at the movie theater. We were groggy at the Freedom House, but we had to get up. It was a day for us to do door-to-door voter registration again.

It was a long day. At the end we got fried chicken and cornbread to go from Milton Hull's Dixie Café (with the advertising slogan "Your Favorite Colored Restaurant") and gathered at the Freedom House. We ate dinner with animated conversation that turned into a meeting to discuss what we had been through and to plan the next day of canvassing. It was well after dark when people went back to the homes where they were staying.

It was my turn to be on guard duty. I was paired with James Hudock for the first shift at the Freedom House. Four students tried to sleep in the middle room. Gunter and another Oberlin student, Dan Cleverdon, went out to patrol the neighborhood in Gunter's car. It was our fourth night in Kosciusko.

Jim had been given a shotgun and I still had the single shot .22 rifle. We tried to spend as much time outside as possible, standing on the front porch or walking on the hillside next to the Freedom House, watching the street and the paths leading through the woods, but it was so cold we kept returning to the front room.

Inside the Freedom House we usually took turns looking out the window toward the street. Sometimes we knelt together by the window, but often one of us took a break and stretched out on a cot. We could have been more cautious. I had no Mississippi street smarts at that time. We had been warned about the threat of an attack, but we didn't know how to recognize a threat.

The night had been quiet for hours. Jim and I were on our knees, peering out each side of the front window, when two carloads of white men drove by in front of the house. One white Ford had two or three white men in it; a second darker car, maybe a Plymouth or an Oldsmobile, passed by packed with more white men. We didn't understand that this was alarming. We didn't warn anyone in the house. We did nothing.

The cars came by a second time, driving more slowly. We simply stared at them through the edges of the window.

"What's going on with these guys? Are they lost?" Jim asked.

"I don't know." I replied. "Seems like they're just driving around looking for something. I don't get it."

Were they actually lost? We still were not alarmed. We still did nothing to alert the other people in the house.

The third time the cars came by very slowly, crawling down the road to the front of the house. They stopped. Paused. Just as Jim and I began to grasp the danger sitting right in front of us, gunfire exploded from the cars. The window we were looking through shattered as buckshot and bullets from an arsenal of shotguns and rifles tore through the house, glass flying, the buckshot ripping through the tar paper walls, bullets piercing the entire front of the house. Don Salisbury was struck in the chest by buckshot as he stood in the open doorway from the middle room, buckling over in pain. James Hudock and I hit the floor as the *bam, bam, bam* of the shotguns mixed with the sharp crack of rifle fire.

I crawled under one of the cots, as time itself seemed to slow down and elongate, stretching like taffy. In slow motion I could see Huddock get off the floor, could see his legs moving to the front door, the door swinging open, and I found myself not thinking, never making a conscious decision, but following the suction of his energy. I got out from under the cot, still clinging to my loaded .22, found my balance, and followed him out the front door. Standing on the wood porch, facing the cars, I raised the rifle to my shoulder. Huddock was already blasting away with his shotgun. In a state of dreamlike calm, despite the chunks of lead whizzing through the air, I took aim, picking a tree just above and in front of the moving white Ford as my target, and lined up the sights on the barrel of the rifle. I took a deep breath, remembering my training. "Don't pull the trigger, squeeze it." Within a second I exhaled, kept my aim and squeezed the trigger. The rifle exploded in my right ear as a bullet pierced the air over the roof of the Ford and hit the tree.

The cars were now speeding away. I had not tried to hit them, not wanting to blow out a tire or shatter a window or do anything that would make them stick around. I wanted them to leave, and they fled. Speeding around the corner, they cut their lights and headed toward a road leading out of town. Gunter and Dan Cleverdon, who had been parked a few blocks away, came tearing down a side street, Gunter driving with his right hand and with his left hand firing a pistol out of the window, Cleverdon firing out of the passenger side. A few more shots rang out, then silence. The attackers were gone.

I don't remember who tended to Don Salisbury. He had been hit just above his heart and now he was lying on the floor, but he wasn't bleeding badly. Dick Klausner had also been hit by a shotgun blast through the window in the middle room as the white men were speeding away, but luckily the buckshot that struck his head just creased his scalp. There was some blood, but Klausner was sitting up, his eyes wide open and his hand pressed against the wound, a look of astonishment on his face.

Gunter returned quickly. "What the hell happened?" he demanded. "Who's hurt? Did you get a good look at the shooters?" The questions kept coming, but our answers were limited. The gunmen were in two cars and no, we didn't realize the risk before the window was shattered by the first shotgun blast. Two of us were wounded, but nobody was badly hurt.

There was no phone at the Freedom House, so Gunter went across the street to use the Nashs' phone. He called the city police and the city hospital. An ambulance arrived and took Don Salisbury away. Four or five neighbors came running over, a few of them older Black men with guns. Albert Truss got there so fast with his rifle that the police initially assumed he had been in the Freedom House when the shots were fired.

The local police spent some time at the house. Once Chief Harvey arrived, there was a serious effort to collect some information. Those of us in Mississippi for the first time expected the local police chief to be hostile, possibly even dangerous. Chief Harvey did not fit our stereotype, except visually, since he was a bit hefty and his uniform fit him loosely. He was cordial as he and another officer questioned the people gathered at the Freedom House and some of the neighbors. He wasn't pleased that we were in his town, but he was irritated that there had been a shooting, particularly with Northern whites being wounded.

As we answered his questions, Huddock and I talked about the two cars, the white Ford and a second car Huddock described as having a maroon bottom and a white top. Most of the neighborhood had heard the shots, but only a few people had seen the cars. Both Eddie Ellis and Frankie Ickom from down the block said they had seen a grey or silver Ford and a maroon and white Plymouth.

Chief Harvey told us that white men in a maroon and white Plymouth had been parked and watching us when we integrated the B&F Grill, and white men in a Ford had watched us at the Strand. He also told us that he had contacted the FBI office in Jackson.

The FBI sent two agents to the Freedom House who arrived around 3 a.m. They came wearing suits and ties and asked to sit down in the front room and talk with everyone. Gunter had them sit on two folding chairs. One was slightly burly, the other reed-thin. Both were well groomed with short-cropped hair. They took clipboards out of their leather cases and looked us over. Gunter had arranged our collection of neighborhood guns on one of the cots, a display meant to send a message that we were well armed. He refused to talk to the agents at all and walked to the back of the house.

Those of us from Oberlin felt torn. We identified ourselves, but all of us had some degree of apprehension about the FBI. I wanted our attackers to be caught, but I had no confidence the FBI shared that goal. It seemed to me the agents were focused on asking about our political affiliations and the identities of our parents. We had grown up in the Red Scare of the fifties and the McCarthy era, and J. Edgar Hoover was still the director of the FBI. He was no friend of the civil rights movement. None of us agreed to be photographed and most of us shared little personal information.

Don Salisbury was already back from the hospital when the agents arrived. They were particularly interested in interviewing him. He was still shaken, bandaged and a bit in shock, but he was willing to speak with the FBI.

After the agents left, some of us stayed awake in the front room. The heater was our only deliverance. While others were able to go back to sleep, Don, Albert Truss, Gunter, Bill Sherzer and I huddled around the heater, smoking cigarettes and talking about what we had just been through. I remember Albert Truss looking very relaxed in denim overalls, leaning back on a wooden crate with his rifle across his knees, a cigarette dangling from his fingers. Sherzer held a pistol on his lap. We passed through that night without another attack.

Gunter amidst Oberlin students. February.
Photo by Peter Westover

The Freedom House in Kosciusko as seen from
the house of Mrs. Pearl Nash and Mr. Edgar Nash.
Photo by the author

Fire at the Freedom House

Chapter 5:
Pecan Pies

The night of the attack I managed only a few hours of sleep. After sitting around the gas stove, I had stretched out on the cot and slept, but people started arriving at the Freedom House early in the morning. Neighbors wanted to know all the details. Oberlin students gathered to talk about the shootings.

Before we could start a meeting, someone came to tell us that there was a phone call for Don Salisbury at the Nash's house. Don had not thought to call his parents, partly because none of us realized that for one day this was a national news story. Don's father was milking the cows on the family farm in upstate New York when he heard on the radio that his son had been shot. He called the MFDP office in Jackson, was given the phone number for Mr. and Mrs. Nash and called immediately. Don went across the street to take the call.

The story was indeed national. News accounts were sent out by the Associated Press and United Press International. John Lewis, at that time chairman of SNCC, issued a statement from Atlanta calling for federal protection for voter registration workers. He sent a telegram to President Johnson that read:

> The Student Nonviolent Coordinating Committee demands the apprehension of the criminals involved in the shooting of civil rights worker Donald Salisbury, 19, of Pulaski, N.Y. in Kosciusko, Miss. We call for an army of 2000 Federal registrars and marshals to be sent into the Black belt of the South to protect those seeking their civil rights and seeking to register voters. If the Federal Government can send hundreds of thousands of troops to Vietnam, the presence of thousands of registrars can be established in the South to insure Freedom. The failure

of the Federal government to ensure the right to vote and to protect the lives of civil rights workers is deplorable. We call for immediate enactment of legislation to make it a Federal crime to take the lives of people involved in obtaining their Constitutional rights and more immediate enforcement of existing legislation.

Our group discussion that morning showed the fear and shock we all shared, as well as our divisions. Some people were very unhappy that any of us had fired guns, even in self-defense. To them it was a fundamental violation of the ethics of a nonviolent movement. Bill Sherzer shared his feelings of regret. "I sat here last night holding a gun. That's not what I believe in, and I won't do it again."

Others, including me, argued that the Black community at this moment of the movement was practicing self-defense, and how could we not be sharing the risks they were taking?

We knew we couldn't resolve the larger issues facing the movement, but we could decide our own course of action. Should we stay for the remainder of winter break or go back to Oberlin? Should we continue to participate in armed self-defense? Leaving now would make the attack a success and place the local civil rights activists more at risk. We overwhelmingly decided to stay.

The question of continuing to participate in armed defense seemed to answer itself. Gunter and Albert Truss and others would already be on guard, and we were free to join them or not. I had already crossed that line and felt comfortable with the decision. Our attackers might return. They were armed and ready to kill. We were armed and ready to die. That difference was our strength.

Meanwhile, the Black students who had worked with us to integrate the restaurants and the movie theater felt the need to do something to respond to the shootings. On their own, the most active students organized a protest march from Tipton High to downtown Kosciusko. More than 100 students walked out of school. The Kosciusko city police blocked the march before anybody could reach the courthouse square, but no-one was arrested.

The Associated Press issued a bulletin titled "Night Riders Hit Civil Rights HQ in Mississippi" which read in part:

Kosciusko, Miss. Feb. 3.

Authorities investigating a nightrider attack on a civil rights headquarters were forced to split their forces today to halt a march into the business district by Negro school children.

Police turned back about 100 young students from the Tipton Street School after they had paraded about three blocks. No incidents were reported.

The hastily mustered group apparently left the school to protest against nightriders firing into a "freedom house" late last night. Two white civil rights workers were slightly injured in the incident.

Local officials said an "intensive investigation" was under way and would continue on an "around the clock" basis until the persons responsible were apprehended. They warned that acts of violence would not be tolerated.

The two FBI agents from Jackson continued to question people. Chief Harvey conducted his own investigation.

We had visitors at the Freedom House all day long. People in the Black community brought plates of food and words of support. Roxie Meredith came by to check on us and brought two pecan pies. She was a short, thin, physically frail woman, but she radiated energy and strength. This was when I learned that Kosciusko was the hometown of James Meredith, who had integrated the University of Mississippi in 1962 in the face of a violent white riot. Roxie Meredith was his mother. She lived on the family land and already knew Gunter and Betty. Her pecan pies were the most intense sweet I had ever tasted, packed with earthy flavor and nourishment.

"Y'all look after yourselves, you hear me?" she admonished us when she left.

A day after the shooting, Mrs. Nash came over to say that my parents had called. I could call them back from her house. It had never occurred to me to call them. I hadn't been shot. Why would I need to talk to my parents?

I followed Mrs. Nash back to her kitchen and made a collect call. My father accepted the charges for the call, which went something like this:

My father: "Are you okay?"

Me: "I'm fine."

My mother, on a separate phone known in those days as an extension: "What do you mean, fine? Just fine? Why haven't you called? What happened?"

I did my best to fumble through an explanation. I gave them a short description of the shooting. No one had been seriously hurt. No, I had not expected to be holding a rifle in Mississippi. Yes, the attackers might be back. I felt safer being armed and, yes, it was my choice.

My parents were not satisfied with my answers. My father was very opposed to guns. "How could you get involved in a shootout? You're in a nonviolent movement."

"Dad, this is the civil rights movement that I'm seeing. People here are armed and have no trouble with the idea of us protecting ourselves."

My mother was focused on my safety. "Why do you want to be there when it's so dangerous? Do you want to get hurt?"

I tried to be reassuring. "No, I don't want to be hurt. Definitely not. That's why I fired back."

This was met with an exasperated sigh. "Call us if anything else happens. Can you promise to do that?"

"Sure, I can promise. Don't worry so much." We left it at that. It was the beginning of a conversation which was never resolved.

I remained on guard duty for one shift every night. Our other organizing work continued. We continued to meet with the students from Tipton High. There was another restaurant integration, without incident. Voter registration remained the primary work. There was still much ground to cover. As we travelled, we watched every car, looking for a two-toned Plymouth and a white Ford.

The night riders did not return that winter. We left Attala County after a few more days of organizing, a bit later than scheduled but in time to get back to school.

I was in one of the last two cars to leave. We drove north to Winona, west to Highway 51 and then straight north to the Tennessee border. Crossing the state line was like coming up for air when you've been held under water far too long. All of us felt a huge sense of relief. We could relax. Breathe.

Fire at the Freedom House

Klausner stopped at the same gas station in Memphis where the attendant had sent us off with the words, "Y'all come back." I imagined the same attendant greeting us with, "Well, y'all made it back. What can I do you for?"

We went inside and loaded ourselves with snacks and drinks. We left when Klausner passed the keys to another driver and got ready to curl up and sleep in the back. We settled in for the long drive to Oberlin, leaving Mississippi behind us. Despite our relief, as we drove away I could already feel a force that held me, like a rubber band stretched over my heart, pulling me back to Mississippi.

Emma Ree Rayford and Shirley Yowk after a meeting
at the Kosciusko Freedom House.
Photo by the author

Chapter 6:
Snow in Oberlin, White Knights in Ethel

We drove into Oberlin so late Sunday night it was already Monday morning, just in time to register for classes. In my packet I found a note from the Dean of Students. I was to report to his office that afternoon.

Dean Adams had an office on the second floor of Peters Hall, an impressive four-story stone building with a tower overlooking Tappan Square. Peters, as we called it, was finished in 1887 with a lavish red oak interior. My hand slid along the smooth wooden bannister as I climbed the staircase to the Dean's office. I felt as though I had been summoned to the heights of college power. James Hudock was already sitting in the waiting room when I arrived.

Together we were brought before Dean Bernard Adams, a pleasant man with a receding hairline and a penchant for smoking a pipe. Seated behind his desk, dressed in a business suit with a white shirt and tie, he was direct with us.

"I understand you two were involved in a gun fight down in Mississippi. Is that correct?"

"Yes, sir."

"Where did you get the guns?"

"They were provided by local people," Jim answered.

"Did you bring any guns back to Oberlin with you?"

"No," I replied as we took turns responding.

"Do you have any guns here on campus?"

"Absolutely not."

"There are no firearms of any kind allowed on campus. Do you understand me?"

"Yes, sir."

"All right. You can go."

That was it. I was a bit disappointed that the Dean had expressed no concern for our safety. Although it was true that the trip was organized by OACR, Oberlin Action for Civil Rights, it was not an official college activity. Still, this was not a very warm welcome.

While it had been bitterly cold in Kosciusko, it was now also freezing in Ohio. It would dip below zero that month, and the ground was often white with snow. White now had a new meaning. As Richard Roisman, a white student who had been with us, wrote about his return to campus in the college newspaper, *The Oberlin Review:*

> By midnight we were back in Ohio, and, although there had not been any noticeable transition at the beginning of our stay, there was a somewhat poignant adjustment to make to Oberlin. I discovered that quite unconsciously in those few short days I had come to view any white stranger as a possible enemy. It took almost a full day in Oberlin for me to stop looking suspiciously at white people.[3]

Roisman also expressed concern about the possibility of white violence directed at the Black community we left behind. More than a few campus activists worried there would be reprisals in Attala County against the high school students. Some of us back at Oberlin were nursing our trembles with no understanding of post-traumatic stress. I, for one, was having trouble concentrating on school, yet all of us were thrown immediately into the routine of attending classes and starting the assigned reading.

We never met as a group after our return to discuss what happened in Kosciusko or to work through how we were feeling. I never fully talked out my experience with any close friends and that seems to have been common among us. Instead, we went on as if everything was normal, despite the fact that it was very difficult to dissect a frog in biology lab or concentrate on a philosophy lecture just days after being in a shoot-out in the dark of night in Mississippi.

The parents of some of the students wrote to the FBI, demanding an investigation into the shooting. In response, parents were notified that "the FBI does not afford protection to civil rights workers." In one instance, the FBI investigated the parents who had written to them. Dan

Cleverdon had been in a car with Gunter at the time of the attack and helped chase the gunmen out of the Black community. His parents were found to be members of the Dobbs Ferry Committee for Human Rights. This fact was duly noted in the FBI report on the shooting.

Other parents wrote to the Justice Department. In response, John Doar, Assistant Attorney General in the Johnson administration, told the parents the federal government could not provide police protection "as the primary responsibility for law and order lies with state and local authorities." At the same time, Doar contacted the FBI in mid-February requesting a full investigation, including "a determination of the kinds of activities in which the victims had engaged and the kinds of such activities for which the Kosciusko Freedom House had been used."

At Oberlin, we were skeptical that there would be any effort to find the gunmen. None of us were contacted by investigators or agents from any law enforcement agency. We didn't know that some efforts were being made to identify the shooters.

In Mississippi, FBI Special Agent William D. Hoskins, based in Jackson, assembled a team of agents to conduct interviews. The report they prepared contains details of conversations with Mr. and Mrs. Nash, Lacey Peeler, Shirley Ann Adams, Willie Lee and others who lived in the neighborhood. Most people had heard the shots, but only Frankie Ickom and Eddie Ellis had seen the cars driven by the attackers. Ellis told the agents that the trunk latch on one of the cars seemed to be broken, because the trunk lid flapped when the car hit a bump. But he made his position clear when he added, "I'm not testifying in no court case. I plan to live in this town, and if I was to be a witness no way I could stay here." [4]

During February and March FBI agents pressured Ickom and Ellis to drive around town with them searching for the two cars. They declined. Many people in the Black community reasonably feared that speaking to the FBI could bring retribution. Civil rights activist Herbert Lee had been shot to death in the Delta town of Liberty in 1961 by white supremacist E.H. Hurst, who claimed self-defense. Louis Allen had witnessed the shooting and tried to tell the FBI that Lee was killed in cold blood, only to be shot to death himself in January of 1964.

Frankie Ickom and Eddie Ellis avoided that fate, but they searched for the cars on their own and believed they located both. They shared this information with Chief Harvey. He traced one car to a man known as Spears, who lived on the outskirts of town with his two sons and may have been one of the white men who watched us from a distance while the B&F Grill was being desegregated. Despite a search warrant, no incriminating evidence was found and Spears was never charged with the shooting.

The FBI had been told by someone who they called "an informant" that there were members of the White Knights in Attala County. The White Knights of the Ku Klux Klan was formed in the early sixties by over 200 Mississippi Klansmen who believed that the other Klan groups in the state, such as the United Klans of America, were too moderate. Under the leadership of Imperial Wizard Sam Bowers, the White Knights promoted the killing of civil rights workers in order "to preserve Christianity and the supremacy of the white race." The group was already linked to at least four murders in the state between 1964 and 1966.

The FBI conducted its own search and found a white Ford that belonged to Pete Shumaker in Kosciusko, whom they had been told was a member of the White Knights. The trunk lid was not broken when they looked at the car. When interviewed, Shumaker denied ever being in the Klan. He claimed that he had been asked to join, but had declined. He refused to name the person who had tried to recruit him to the Klan. Kosciusko residents Haywood Chandler and Herbert King also denied any involvement with the Klan.

The informant told the FBI that there was a chapter of the White Knights in the town of Ethel, ten miles northeast of Kosciusko. The agents shifted their attention to Ethel and visited a list of individuals identified by the informant.

Colon Beck of Ethel denied being in the Klan. Wayne Mitchell Proctor told the agents a man named Rank Boyte had asked him to join the White Knights of the Ku Klux Klan. Proctor said he told Boyte he did not want to join.

James Black of Ethel told the FBI he was not a member of the Klan and had never attended a Klan meeting. According to the FBI, James Black told the agents that "he believes in the supremacy of the white race and believes this is one of the good objectives of the Klan." He said he was at a church meeting in Ethel on the night of the Freedom House shooting.

A different story emerged from Robert Lewis Steed, who placed James Black at a meeting of the White Knights in Neshoba County. According to the FBI report on Robert Steed:

> When questioned concerning his relationship to the Klan, he advised that he was a member of the White Knights of the Ku Klux Klan of Mississippi in the early part of 1965. He said when he realized that this organization at times professed acts of violence, he left the organization and has had no contact with it since the end of spring in 1965.
>
> He advised that the person who first contacted him and asked him to join the Klan was a Baptist minister named Rank Boyte. He said he attended one meeting in Philadelphia, Mississippi, with Rank Boyte and James Black but said he does not recall anyone else who was at that meeting. He further stated he attended two meetings in Ethel, Mississippi. He said one meeting was at the house of Howard Turner and the other was at the house of Colon Belk. The only other person he remembers being at the meetings in Ethel was Pete Shumaker of Kosciusko, Mississippi.

The unnamed informant, however, provided cover for the local White Knights of Ethel. He told the FBI that he "personally can account for the whereabouts of most of the Ethel unit on the night of the shooting as they were attending a church meeting on the night of February 2, 1966 and were in his presence."

This provided an alibi not only for the group but also for the informant, and was apparently sufficient for the Special Agents to close their file. Despite a memo from John Doar to the FBI on May 12, 1966, again requesting a full investigation, nothing further was done.

The concern at Oberlin that our burst of activity in Kosciusko would lead to more violence after we left was unfounded. Instead, the movement in Attala County gained strength. During those months Betty Jones returned to Kosciusko from Vicksburg and worked with Gunter to build the MFDP. The student group at Tipton High continued to organize and legal assistance continued to be provided from Jackson.

During that semester, while sitting in class or walking across campus, I felt some visceral connection pulling me back to the Deep South. I wanted to be working with the movement, walking dirt roads and talking with people on the porches of their wooden shacks, not sitting in some lecture hall taking notes. My drive to be a civil rights worker in the South was a calling, and it had not been fulfilled. What was I doing in school?

One reason for staying was the threat of the draft. At that time all men were subject to compulsory military service at age 18. The war in Vietnam was raging. There was no lottery system yet, just a patchwork of temporary deferments and permanent exemptions. Ministers, conscientious objectors and those who failed the physical examination could be exempt. Full-time students were given a deferment, so as long as you stayed in school you were fine.

This was a serious problem for male organizers in the Deep South, both Black and white. One Oberlin student, David Owen, despite being brutally beaten in Hattiesburg during Freedom Summer in 1964, dropped out of school to remain in the Mississippi civil rights movement. Instead, he was ordered to take a military physical, and when he passed he was promptly drafted. Many local male activists faced the possibility of being drafted as soon as they graduated from high school.

The number of young men being drafted was on the rise in 1966. I was eager to return to Mississippi as soon as possible, but realistically that meant returning no earlier than at the end of the school year, in early June. If I lost my student deferment, I'd be in the military, not in Mississippi.

I wrote to the MFDP office in Jackson from my dormitory room asking if there was going to be a summer program that year. I received the following letter:

> April 26, 1966:
> Dear Mr. Rinaldi,
>
> Thank you for writing me concerning your interest in working in Mississippi this summer.
>
> We are now in the process of sending out applications and information pertinent to our summer program. You should expect to hear from our office around the first of May.

Fire at the Freedom House

Since you already have parental consent I would suggest that you enclose it when you return the summer application.

Looking forward to meeting you.

Yours in freedom,

Lawrence T. Guyot

Chairman

MFDP

Letter from the Mississippi Freedom Democratic Party.

I knew from the moment that letter arrived I would be returning to Mississippi. I stayed at Oberlin, even though it became even more difficult to concentrate on schoolwork. One unexpected benefit of staying on campus was the tapestry of friendships which developed that year. Young and new to being away from our parents, we bonded through shared experiences and endless hours of conversation.

I next heard from the MFDP when I received a letter sent on May 21, informing me that a training session would take place in Atlanta. The date was not yet set and there was no application form enclosed. Instead, the letter came with a brochure for the MFDP Summer Program for 1966. It announced voter registration drives, freedom schools and plans to run candidates in all Congressional Districts, with particular emphasis on Madison, Jefferson and Sunflower counties.

This was not Freedom Summer, in magnitude or impact, but it was similar in concept. It was a call from Mississippi for Northern students to be civil rights workers for the summer. We would go through formal training and then be sent out to the local organizing projects. I was being invited to return.

The semester dragged on. Final exams began on Tuesday, May 31. Had I even gone to the lectures or the labs? Had I forgotten some class entirely?

In the midst of finals I turned 19 and my friend Wendy Forbush took me out for ice cream. We bought cones at the local ice cream shop and sat crossed-legged together on the soft grass in Tappan Square. "You still going South?" she asked. "Seems pretty certain," I replied. Neither of us mentioned the dangers that lay ahead. She gave me her parents' phone number in Baltimore and told me to call.

Saturday was my last exam. I said good-bye to my other campus friends, who were scattering for the summer, and left for New York. First semester of freshman year I had made Dean's List. This semester I earned my first D. It was a relief to be done.

I reached Valley Stream on Sunday, June 5. There still was no word about the formal training for the summer program. I called the Jackson office and was told that the training was now uncertain and I should just come down.

I had arrived home in time for the final week of preparations for my sister's wedding. Jane was marrying a man she had met in graduate school. Dave was a thin, quiet fellow who was getting a PhD. in physics. The ceremony was scheduled for Saturday, June 11. With the help of a travel agent, I booked a flight to Jackson for the next day.

The wedding ceremony was meant to be simple, but few weddings are simple and this was no exception. All week we got ready. I bought wedding clothes and got a haircut. My parents handled the demands of food and housing for family and guests and helped my sister with an array of decisions. My grandmothers spent the week cooking.

I used the time to get ready for my return South. Since everyone's focus was on the wedding, there was little talk about my civil rights work. The marriage was a wonderful diversion. I already had a signed parental consent form, so it was easy for me to avoid bringing up the topic of Mississippi.

My parents still found time to express their fear for my safety, especially my mother. She was particularly worried about a return to Kosciusko. She questioned why I needed to go back to a place where people had shot at me. "How can you put us through this again?" she said. I replied that I was returning to work with the MFDP and I had no idea where I would be sent. The summer brochure talked about work in Sunflower, Jefferson and Madison counties. My work might not be in Kosciusko and might not even involve carrying a gun. That seemed to help, at least a little.

Relatives started arriving by the end of the week, many from Brooklyn and New Jersey. Some of my favorite cousins came to participate. All of our attention was now focused on the wedding. My sister and Dave were married at a Unitarian Church on Long Island, with a reception catered at the church after the ceremony.

There was no grand pageantry, as I had seen at Roman Catholic weddings in my family. Though my sister wore a flowing white wedding gown with a white tiara and Dave and his best man wore tuxedos, the Unitarian chapel seemed like a small high school auditorium. The reception was held with folding chairs at long tables and a catered meal that featured turkey, mashed potatoes with gravy and a side of vegetables.

This food was embellished with some of my grandmothers' delicacies, antipasto overflowing with peppers, cheeses, salami and anchovies, handmade ravioli, Italian stuffed artichokes and mushroom caps with chopped stems, bread crumbs, herbs, olive oil and parmesan cheese. Embraced by a happy, protective family, gentle dance music in the background, I could close my eyes and float on a cloud of relaxation and peace.

The next morning I flew to the small airport in Jackson. I was told someone would be waiting for me.

Membership Card
MISSISSIPPI FREEDOM DEMOCRATIC PARTY
This is to certify that

Mr.
Miss
Mrs. _____ MATTHEW JAMES RINALDI _____
is a member in good standing and is entitled to full participation in all activities, elections, benefits and privileges afforded by the Constitution and By-laws of the Party.

Mrs. Annie Devine

Mrs. Annie Devine, Secretary, February 21, 1965

I pledge $ _____ annually to support the programs and activities of the Mississippi Freedom Democratic Party.

MEMBERSHIP IN THE MISSISSIPPI FREEDOM DEMOCRATIC PARTY, a political organization loyal to the platform and principles of the National Democratic Party is open to all adult residents of the state of Mississippi regardless of race, color or creed.

Because the oppressive policies and discriminatory practices of the state of Mississippi deprive the majority of Negroes of the right to vote, membership in the M.F.D.P. is not dependent on whether or not an individual is registered to vote under present conditions.

All members of the Party are eligible to stand for and to hold any or all positions and offices in the Party.

It is the duty and responsibility of all members to attend and participate in all precinct, district and county meetings, to contribute to the formulation of all policies and programs and to vote in all elections in the Party.

Chapter 7:
Back in Harm's Way

The first time I had traveled to Mississippi with veteran civil rights workers. Now I was arriving alone. I needed someone to appear and take care of me. As I walked into the airport terminal a Black man in his thirties or forties made eye contact. Any eye contact with a stranger, in any setting, can be fraught with misunderstanding. Interracial eye contact in this setting was a risk if you were Black and somewhat startling if you were white. I looked the man back in the eyes, hoping he was the person there to meet me. He approached me and knew my name. I smiled with relief.

Had I been that obvious? Was I wearing a sign around my neck that said "Yankee"? In preparation for returning I had shaved the beard I had grown in the past few months. I had gotten a haircut for the wedding. I thought I would blend in, at least at the airport. Instead, this man seemed to have easily picked me out. He led me out of the small airport to his parked car. I don't remember much conversation as he drove me to the MFDP on North Farish Street in Jackson. I do remember climbing a wooden staircase to the office and parting from this man who I would not see again for months.

The office was a buzz of sound and activity, phones ringing, people involved in multiple conversations, a huge map of the state on the wall with pins in it and notes pointing in every direction. When our group had arrived in January, the office had been hectic with plans for the Poor People's Conference. Now, the MFDP was pouring its energy into supporting the march begun a week earlier by James Meredith.

Meredith, famous for integrating Ole Miss in 1962, had initiated his own one-man march on Sunday, June 5, designed to call attention to the right of all Mississippians to register and vote. He hoped that showing his own courage could help others overcome their fear. The route for the

Meredith March Against Fear was to be from Memphis to Jackson, but on Monday, June 6, barely 15 miles after crossing the Mississippi state line, James Meredith was shot.

A white gunman hiding in ambush fired multiple blasts from a shotgun. Meredith hit the ground bleeding. His wounds were serious and painful, but fortunately not fatal. He was hospitalized and the gunman soon captured. I knew Roxie Meredith must be worried back in Kosciusko. A coalition of major civil rights organizations soon stepped forward to resume his march, now widely known simply as the Meredith March.

There was precedent for such a singular undertaking. In 1963 William Moore, a white member of CORE who worked as a postal carrier in Baltimore, took vacation time to stage a one-man march to Jackson, where he planned to deliver a letter to Mississippi Gov. Ross Barnett supporting integration. He was shot dead near Gadsden, Alabama. At least 15 veteran civil rights workers, including Freedom Rider Diane Nash, took up William Moore's march. All were arrested, some multiple times, and the march was crushed. Now, in 1966, with more focus and resources, the movement was again taking up the march of an ambushed activist.

The MFDP office staff was busy coordinating planning and logistics. I stood around until someone brought me to speak with Lawrence Guyot. He was very warm and welcoming and made it clear that they were totally consumed by the Meredith March. He said the MFDP wanted me for the summer program and not for the march. They would find me a place to stay in Jackson that night. I could wait to be placed in an organizing project. Any talk of training the summer volunteers was forgotten. I later learned that a telegram had been sent to my dormitory at Oberlin from Hosea Williams telling me the summer project training had been delayed to June 15, but it hardly mattered since I was already in Mississippi. The training never happened. At the same time a form letter from Hosea Williams and Martin Luther King had also been sent to my dormitory. It read:

> Dear Freedom Fighters:
> The dastardly shooting of James Meredith has com-
> pelled the Southern Christian Leadership Conference to
> join SNCC, CORE and other organizations to continue his

march in support of Negro voter registration and against the crippling fear which has so long enslaved our brothers in Mississippi.

All lovers of Freedom are urged to report to the Centenary Methodist Church, 878 Mississippi Boulevard, Memphis, Tennessee. This church is serving as headquarters for the march. Transportation will be available from the church to the march in progress.

Please join us in this historic effort.

For freedom,

Martin Luther King, Jr.

Hosea L. Williams

By June 14th the march had veered into the Delta and was still well north of Jackson. I knew nothing about the call for Black Power raised by SNCC activists, which would profoundly impact the movement. I did know something from my membership in CORE about the growing disagreements among the major civil rights organizations over issues like armed self-defense and the participation of whites. As far as I knew, the leaders had worked to put those differences aside for the moment.

I never considered joining the march, which might last for weeks. The march was important and the people who participated risked everything. I was ready to take similar risks, but I had come back to be an organizer "in the field," the phrase used by the movement to mean activists who lived and worked in the rural Black communities. The MFDP was in favor of the inclusion of whites in the summer program, and, unofficially, of self-defense. I was willing to go anywhere they sent me.

Waiting to be placed, I spent three nights in Jackson. The first night the MFDP sent me to the house of a group of white women working with the Medical Committee for Human Rights. There was plenty to talk about, since at least half of the women were planning to leave. Apparently the director of the Medical Committee, Dr. Alvin Poussaint, had given a speech arguing that white women were coming South to live out a fantasy they had seen in the movies, that of a white woman living amidst an African tribe and being idolized for her white skin. Dr. Poussaint called it "The White African Queen Syndrome." The speech was soon to be published as a paper in *the American Journal of Psychiatry*. The women in the house were offended and worried. Some had decided they were done with the movement. "Hey guy," one of them said to me, "the times they are a changin', and our time here is over. White people are not wanted anymore. You won't be here long."

Could they be right? There were swirling issues of race and gender tearing at the bonds within the movement. Some longtime activists felt that the original vision of the movement as "the beloved community" had vanished. Yet I had been encouraged by the Black leadership of the MFDP to return and I wanted to be here.

At the office the next morning the staff was again reassuring. It was made clear that no matter what else was happening in the movement, the MFDP wanted me to stay, even though they had still not decided where to send me. The personal relationships I experienced in the office were still the interracial harmony of the beloved community, but the movement in many counties was straining to keep up with the Meredith March planning and could not take on supervising an unknown white organizer. The office was busy with more pressing tasks, and placing me in the field could wait.

There was a decision to extract me from the turmoil in the Medical Committee. I was moved to another house in Jackson. I spent the next two days with an older Black woman, a staunch supporter of the MFDP. I could not have hoped for a better host. She was warm and made me feel at home, though she did look me earnestly in the eye and ask, "Son, how old are you?" When I told her I was 19, she shook her head. "You're so young," she said quietly, "So young." I didn't feel young. At that time I could walk into a bar in New York and have a beer. I thought I was an adult.

I spent the next day doing odd jobs in the office, mostly stuffing envelopes. There was still no hint where I might be sent. Attala County was not my focus. I had not kept in touch with Gunter. I knew he had faults, despite the fact that he was playing a heroic role. He loved his guns, had a reputation for "shooting at anything" and could disappear for hours at a time with no explanation. I was not planning on a return to Attala County, but I was eager to get started somewhere.

On the third day someone on staff had the time to sit with me and focus on getting me out in the field. It didn't take long to place me. "Oh, you were with the group that went to Kosciusko last winter. How do you feel about self-defense?" I told the staff person about the details of the shooting in February and that I was comfortable with what I had done. A phone call from the office to Gunter quickly got me placed. He drove to Jackson and picked me up that afternoon.

Gunter made an impression on everyone in the room as soon as he walked in the door. The man was tall. Long and thin with his dungarees still drooping from his hips, his gaze swept over the room like a hawk gliding over a hillside. He greeted me by name, spoke with a few people in the office and with a nod of his head let me know it was time to leave.

I felt exhilarated to be leaving the city. Three mostly idle days in Jackson had been enough. Though I felt uneasy with Gunter at first, I felt good about returning to the community where our group had been during the winter and looked forward to working again with so many courageous people in Kosciusko. I remembered the tremendous energy of the high school students, the many families ready to care for us and especially Mrs. Nash, who had been so nurturing.

A few miles north of Jackson, Gunter turned east off Highway 51 and headed to the Natchez Trace. The Trace, as it was known, was a two-lane road curling through wooded swamps and crossing open farmland, following a foot trail first used by the Choctaw people. It stretched from the land of the Natchez people on the Mississippi River to the land of the Chickasaw in the north, serving as a trading route among the indigenous people. The trail between Jackson and the central hills followed creeks and high ground along the Pearl and Yockanookany Rivers. Now the old footpath was a strip of asphalt with a white line down the middle, leading me back to a community of descendants of African slaves.

At first Gunter and I barely spoke. The windows were rolled down in the summer humidity and heat, cooling us off and leaving me free to take in the land around us. Grassy green meadows were surrounded by forests of pine and cypress trees, their branches covered by light green Spanish moss. At times a river appeared through the trees on the right, forested on both sides. At times the road led through swampland, where I had my first view of the dense, mucky stands of water that looked like a flooded forest. Living cypress trees grew in these dark waters next to stumps of rotting trees sticking up through the shimmering surface. We drove almost 70 miles without passing through a town. A few scattered farmhouses appeared, set back in the meadows. A few tractors and hay balers sat absorbing the heat of the sun.

The Trace, heading northeast, led to a series of small towns and small cities, to Tupelo and Corinth and finally to the Tennessee border. Between Jackson and Attala County you had to take an exit off the main road to reach any towns or small communities. The left turn to Kosciusko was just past Holly Hill and Red Dog Road. If you got to Hurricane Creek you had gone too far.

Although we were travelling in broad daylight, I soon found my exhilaration tempered by feelings of fear, a watchfulness and hyper-alertness I had first experienced and internalized during the winter. Were we being followed on the Natchez Trace? No. There was barely any traffic, and there was nothing particular about us to attract attention, just two white guys in a beat-up old car with a Mississippi license plate. I didn't feel in any immediate danger, but some internal alarm signal had been switched on. There was tension in my muscles and tightness in my chest. My shoulders were hunched and all my senses became alert and focused.

Gunter finally did strike up a conversation. He knew I was one of the students who had fired back at the attackers when our group had been in Kosciusko during the winter. That certainly was one reason he had agreed to take me on. He told me about work in the county since we left. Betty Jones had returned and lived with him at the Freedom House. At the moment she was again visiting her family in Vicksburg and might join the Meredith March. He asked about my days in Jackson and my plans for the summer. I told him I was planning on returning to Oberlin in the fall. He probably saw me as a privileged white kid with the money to go to a private college.

There was a turn in our conversation.

"How much money did you bring with you?"

"A little over $150," I replied. "I figured on a budget of about $10 a week." This seemed reasonable, since this was the standard pay for civil rights workers in the field.

"Give it to me and I'll hold it for you," he said.

"Naw, I don't need you to handle it for me. Anyway, most of it is in Travelers Checks, so I want to hold on to them."

Fire at the Freedom House

"How much cash do you have?"

"I don't know exactly. Twenty or thirty dollars."

"Give me ten bucks for gas."

How could I refuse? He was giving me a ride out of Jackson, and I would be dependent on him once we got to Attala County. I handed over the cash. He took it in hand, leaned back in his seat and pushed it into a pocket of his dungarees. I had the uncomfortable realization, no surprise really, that I would have to be watchful of Gunter as well.

Luther Mallet on the porch of the Freedom House.
Photo by Matthew Rinaldi

Chapter 8:
Meeting Luther

We continued driving the Trace in relative silence. Gunter never revealed much about himself, at least not to me. He did not need to talk all the time, which made it easy for me to be around him. Being quiet was a useful skill in Mississippi. Listening was important.

We arrived in Kosciusko in the late afternoon, as it began to cool down. An exit lane from the Natchez Trace led through a lightly wooded pine forest on the edge of town, and with two more turns we were off the asphalt and onto a dirt road leading to the Black community. We drove by houses and shacks spaced among the pine trees, well-worn trails leading through the forest. It felt wonderfully familiar. One more turn and we were at the Freedom House, just four months after the tumultuous days in January and February. It wasn't winter anymore. The sun had been blazing all day, the air was muggy and the dirt roads were packed dry. It helped that I had grown up on the East Coast with no air-conditioning, but this was hotter than a hot summer in New York. I was looking forward to the cool breeze that came with sunset.

The Freedom House hadn't changed, three small rooms set in a straight row front to back, a wooden frame, walls of tar paper. The front porch was still set on cinderblocks, though the block on one side was leaning downhill more severely than four months earlier. It was a wonder that porch didn't just give in and slide down the hill. Four wooden steps up to the porch led to the front door and the front window. Above the front window was the same sign, the painted black lettering on the window frame proclaiming boldly and in capital letters: FREEDOM HOUSE.

Standing on that porch was a person I didn't recognize. A young Black man, maybe younger than me, in dungarees and a short-sleeved shirt, wearing a straw hat set at a jaunty angle. He looked fit and trim and very self-confident.

"This is Luther Mallett," Gunter said. "Luther just graduated from Tipton High. He was active when we integrated the restaurants. So were his brother Wiley and his sister Jean. They're a strong family."

Luther had a warm smile for me. "Glad to meet you. Welcome back to Miss'ippi. I don't think we ever met when you were here."

"No, I don't think so. I'm Matt. Glad to meet you."

We shook hands for the first time. His grip was strong.

The three of us went inside. Gunter gave me the front cot, the same one I'd had in the winter. He had the back room as his private room. Not a problem for me. I dumped my duffle bag on the floor and unrolled my sleeping bag, spreading it out on the canvas cot.

The room was much the same, though it had been cleaned up a bit. It was comfortable being inside; the shade of the building made it cooler. The gas heater sat by the wall, but we didn't need it now. There were still bullet holes in the walls from the shooting in February, but the front window had been repaired and was once again solid glass instead of makeshift boards.

There were two changes that I noticed right away. The first was that there was now a telephone. It sat on a small table near the other cot in

Matthew Rinaldi on the porch of the Freedom House.
Photo by Luther Mallett

Fire at the Freedom House

the front room. There were piles of paper on the floor and the edge of the cot could function as a desk, so that made it a small office of sorts. The second change, more visually striking, was the addition on one wall of a full-color recruiting poster for the White Knights, with a robed and hooded Klansman emerging from an image of Uncle Sam taking off his hat. "I Want You in the White Knights of Mississippi Ku Klux Klan" it proclaimed.

"What's with that?" I asked.

Luther laughed as Gunter quickly responded. "Don't you touch my poster," he said firmly. "I took it off a wood fence and I haven't seen another one like it since."

I could understand. The poster hung there like a trophy, like a captured battle flag.

We chatted for a while, and I learned that Gunter and Luther had been taking down or painting over KKK signs throughout the county at night. We talked until one of the neighbors came to tell us it was time to eat. Luther and Gunter didn't seem surprised, and I was certainly hungry. We followed a dirt path that led to an outdoor table stacked with plates of food. A few people were already there, including some of the high school activists we had worked with during the winter. These people were among the core of the local movement, Black people who looked at white people directly, who had dropped the veneer of deference and accepted white civil rights workers as equals in their community. I was introduced around. People looked me in the eye and shook my hand and seemed genuinely glad to see me.

Dinner was a feast. Fried chicken, yams, collard greens, black-eyed peas, cornbread and lots of ice-cold sweet tea, followed by a dessert of sweet potato pie. I knew enough from my time in the winter to recognize this as a feast, nobody's regular dinner, and I appreciated the welcome. Luther sat next to me on the wooden bench, cheerful and talkative and happy to be eating. I felt comfortable with him already. He was outwardly respectful of the adults, playful with the children and funny when he joked with his friends.

After dinner we chatted a bit more, then Luther took off for his home. Gunter brought me across the road to Mrs. Nash, who welcomed me back and let me know I could again wash up and use the bathroom at her house any time. I thanked her, very glad to see her again. It was hot and muggy, but it was a soothing country heat in clean air after three nights in gritty Jackson. After cleaning up at the Nash's I crossed the road and was soon sound asleep on the cot.

The next morning started slowly. I'd had a good night's rest. Gunter was already gone, leaving a note that simply said, "I'm out." I crossed over to Mrs. Nash's to wash and change, then walked around the corner to Izah Brown's little kitchen and grocery store for another welcome back and breakfast.

When I returned to the Freedom House the car was back. Gunter had arrived with Luther, who greeted me warmly. The three of us went inside to talk about what we would focus on that summer. Gunter made it clear that being a part of the project, a term used to describe an outpost of the movement, meant being involved on a full-time basis and being ready to take risks we would not ask of others. Luther and I were both ready to make that commitment.

Gunter and Betty had started the project in Kosciusko together in 1965. They had both worked with CORE and had met as paid staff with a Head Start program run through the Delta Ministry. These similarities in our backgrounds, though in very different settings, helped us bond. Gunter was sure Betty would be back soon. When she returned the four of us would work as a unit, each of us responsible to each other every day, all day long. We would be relying on each other for survival.

"We're expendable," said Gunter. "Betty taught me that. People come and go. I see it all the time. We're catalysts. What we do is meaningless if we don't build a local organization. Here and now that means building the MFDP."

That all made sense to me. There was a local MFDP structure, a network of residents who agreed on the long-term strategy, which was to build Black voting power in the county and the state. Voter registration was fundamental. If more Black residents were registered, it would empower the entire community. Doing voter registration work was also an easy way to go house to house, an easy first opening to a conversation. It was the way to meet people. Gunter and Betty had been concentrating on the area within the city limits of Kosciusko since the autumn of 1965, and by now a few hundred people in the Black community had registered.

This was a significant start in a county with around four thousand voters and perhaps two thousand more eligible Black adults.

There were only estimates of the number of Black voters in the state, and they varied, but all of them were encouraging. In 1960 the numbers in Mississippi were 8,000 to 10,000 registered voters of African descent. By 1964 the estimates had risen to 30,000 to 60,000 registrants. Estimates rose as high as 117,000 to over 175,000 registered Black voters in 1966. Each registration was an act of courage. Each vote that was cast was another step toward dismantling the existing power structure, particularly at the local level.

In Kosciusko the party was growing as well. The local committee of the MFDP was expanding. In January the Jackson office had only Gunter's name and the Nash phone number as the contact in Attala County. After February a group of local leaders stepped forward and Dock Drummond, J.P. Presley, and Susie Bell were added to the contact list. This meant that local people now had access to the resources of the larger movement, including legal services.

Gunter and Betty and the MFDP in Jackson and people locally were also ready to move beyond voter registration. There had already been sit-ins at the restaurants and the movie theater in Kosciusko. Throughout the winter Betty and Gunter had also worked on a boycott of stores that did not hire Black people. Now, Gunter said, was the time to move against all the public spaces that were segregated, the parks and the roadside stores, the bathrooms at the gas stations as well as the spaces that were "whites only" like the only city swimming pool.

It was also clear that it was time to give more attention to the small towns and rural areas in Attala County outside Kosciusko.

Luther and I both said we were ready for all those challenges. Luther had just graduated from high school and was ready to commit himself to this work. I was the college student, planning to go back to college sometime in September,

but I was committed to the movement and knew there was no predicting what might happen to us.

At some point in our conversation a city police car drove up on the road in front of the Freedom House. It was Chief of Police Herbert Harvey, come to pay a visit. As a lawman he was a keeper of the peace, a police chief who didn't want there to be any trouble. He had come to see which of those college students had returned to his town. He and Gunter talked on the front lawn, such as it was, for a few minutes. Luther kept his distance but sat outside on the porch. When the police chief nodded at him in recognition, Luther looked him in the eyes and nodded right back. At one point Gunter called me over.

"So," Chief Harvey said to me, "what brings you back to Kosciusko?"

"Well, I'm here to work with the civil rights movement."

"Is that so? I sure hope you're not here to stir up trouble. I want to keep this town nice and quiet."

This was followed by some conversation about the County Sheriff, Al Malone, who was a force unto himself and might not be as kindly disposed to outsiders. I got the drift, said I understood, and went back to the porch. It was easier to sit with Luther and let Gunter deal with the police chief. They chatted for another five or ten minutes.

Luther filled me in on Sheriff Malone. He was law enforcement in the small towns and rural areas of Attala County outside of Kosciusko and, according to Luther, he was friendly with men in the white community who were likely to resent our work. "He's a man who'll remember your face," Luther cautioned. The sheriff also had some complicated relationship with the local bootleggers, possibly collecting payments from them. Attala County was dry at that time and was set to vote in August on whether to allow the legal sale of alcohol.

Gunter and Chief Harvey finished their conversation and parted with nods but without shaking hands. "Time to get moving," Gunter announced after the police chief had driven away.

"Where to?"

"Time for some target practice."

I had conflicted feelings. Target practice can be fun, like shooting at clay targets at a county fair, but my instant thought was that I was being tested. I carried that thought with me as we got ready.

We loaded up the car with some of the little arsenal in the Freedom House, one or two pistols, two shotguns, that .22 caliber rifle, boxes of shells. Everything was put out in plain view. It was my understanding that carrying a concealed weapon without a permit was illegal. Of course we could always be charged with anything at any time, but that was no reason to break this particular law. The laws we intentionally broke were the laws related to white supremacy.

We got in the car and drove, Gunter behind the wheel. I had no idea where we were going, but it was comforting to be on the road as part of a group of three. The forests and the kudzu plants we passed filled me with wonder. Kudzu is a climbing green vine that seemed to cover the hillsides. Every so often, I saw a magnolia tree in bloom, its glossy thick leaves giving birth to huge fragrant white flowers. At some point we took a dirt driveway to a clearing with empty soda cans and tobacco tins strewn on the ground. Gunter parked the car and we unloaded the guns.

Gunter set up some cans and metal tins on the top of an old fence, then handed me the .22 rifle. That was a relief. These were easy shots for me. At the Mount Hermon rifle range I had excellent training, and most of my shots sent a can flying. This was a moment of affirmation. It was clear that Gunter and Luther were pleased. When it was Luther's turn with the rifle I don't think he missed a single shot.

Trying to use the pistols was something else again.

"You ever fired a pistol?" Gunter wanted to know.

"Never."

"Ever had one in your hands?"

"Never."

And it showed. I think I fired all six rounds in the revolver without hitting a thing. I knew basic safety rules, so I never pointed the barrel at anything other than the target or the ground, but I was a lousy shot with a handgun. I didn't know how to hold it and my hand trembled. Gunter was mildly disgusted. Luther was more charitable, though when it was his turn, he put holes in the cans with most of his shots. We tried a few more rounds, and I think I finally managed to hit one old tin can with a .38 Smith & Wesson. There was a thrill to all this shooting and to seeing the tin can fly when it was hit. There is something fun and empowering about guns, which masks the terrible damage they can do.

But really, what was the point of handguns? To me, the point of being armed was to discourage an attack, and the best way to announce that you were armed was holding a very visible rifle. More than anything, I knew that being armed was very different from curling up in a fetal position and letting some white man stomp on me. Gunter knew that I had returned fire in February, and Luther was impressed that this college kid could even use a gun. I had their trust, and now I had the .22 rifle as well.

We spent the rest of the daylight hours visiting in the Black community. I think Gunter's goal was to let people know that someone from the winter group had returned, to show me to the community and to show more of the community to me. We dropped in at Presley's Barber Shop for a brief hello. We stayed for maybe half an hour at Bell's Pool Hall, a dark space even on a summer afternoon. A few players were grouped around tables, one or two wearing cotton muscle shirts glistening with sweat. Despite the heat it was an easy place to stand around, just to be seen.

We also stopped at the Black-owned auto repair shop near the cemetery. Housed in a worn cement-block building, the repair shop seemed reasonably well equipped and the mechanic who talked with us appeared quite confident. This was very important. We had to keep the car running and we had to avoid breaking down somewhere outside the city, on a back road in some rural part of the county. The mechanic was a man in his thirties who had a feel for machines. The car never broke down on us.

Dinner was some leftovers stashed at the Freedom House. I thought we were pretty much done for the day, but Gunter had one more event in mind. After we ate he picked up two cans of spray paint from the back room and the three of us headed out in the car, the sun setting, the air cooling off. Luther explained that they had seen a Klan sign on a small bridge, but it was daylight when they passed the sign and they had no paint with them at the time. In about 15 minutes we were at the bridge. While Luther and I kept a watchful eye on the road, Gunter turned the KKK sign into nothing but a blob of black paint. It was our goal to eliminate any form of intimidation by the Klan, including any indication it was active in the county, and ultimately to eliminate the Klan's power over people's lives. That night we slept well.

Chapter 9:
Sitting by the River

The next day Luther and I went out as a pair for the first time. Luther had an old pickup truck his mom let us borrow. He drove us to an area of small farms north of Kosciusko. Since he knew the back roads, he kept us on dirt and away from most of the traffic.

Much of the land was being cultivated by small farmers. This was not a county of large plantations. Most farms were owned by white families who either worked the land themselves or used sharecroppers. Many Black farmers were tenant farmers or sharecroppers who paid white landowners with a portion or "share" of their crop. Attala County was also home to a few hundred Black landowners, a substantial number in Mississippi. Land ownership brought a small measure of safety and influence, so as a group, Black landowners in Attala County added that strength to the local civil rights movement.

We visited perhaps five to seven different homes that day. Some of the houses were small wooden shacks, usually inhabited by sharecroppers. Some of the houses were more substantial, with solid walls and comfortable furniture. All the people we visited shared a common heritage as the descendants of enslaved people who had been brought to Mississippi by whites from other states.

Luther and I found that we worked well together. We both carried voter registration forms and encouraged people to exercise the right to register. We easily deferred to each other. I was glad that Luther was full of energy and was taking the lead. I think the very act of having two young people, one Black and one white, treating each other as equals, at your house, on your porch, carried with it the visceral message that the future could indeed be different.

Luther and I made it a slow day. It was hot and we never rushed our visits. One young couple were already registered to vote and were supporters of the MFDP. They invited us inside for sandwiches and tea. We lingered as we talked about what was happening with the civil rights movement and savored the cool shade and the cold tea.

After we visited two more farms, we found ourselves on a bridge crossing a small river. Time for another break. We parked the truck on an open patch of ground and sat by the edge of the river with an unobstructed view of any cars that might travel down the road. Our legs dangled over the water, but we kept our shoes on, just in case we needed to run back to the truck. It was quiet in the afternoon sun.

We talked, mostly about our families at first. I learned that Luther lived with his mother and three younger siblings on a small farm they owned on the edge of town. He had just finished high school. His father was gone, and his older sister, Leila Mae, had left Mississippi, part of the migration north.

"Your parents alive?" he asked. "You got any brothers or sisters?"

"Both my mother and father live outside New York City. I have one sister, about four years older than me. She just got married."

"Where's she at?"

"She lives near Boston."

I was describing a world that Luther had to imagine.

Then we started talking about girls, and with that our worlds were suddenly similar. We certainly shared a common interest. Luther was keeping company with more than one young lady from Tipton High and his life was getting complicated.

"You know, Matt, it can be tough being with more than one girl at a time. Sometimes a girl can get so jealous she's ready to scream. I'll tell you – it works out better if they don't know about each other."

"How can that work out? This is a pretty small place."

"Well, you gotta expect that they be doing the same thing. You start getting really serious about one girl, you probably best be getting married."

"Anybody you're that serious about?"

He laughed. "No, not yet. How about you?"

I told him about a high school girlfriend. I told him that there were girls I was attracted to at college, but the girl who was really my best friend, Wendy, was the girlfriend of one of the leaders of the campus civil rights movement.

"You heard from her?"

"Oh, for sure. She writes and we talk on the phone. Really, she's a good friend."

We both paused as a car passed by on the road. There was a Black man behind the wheel, and he waved to us.

Luther thought for a moment and then said, "Matt, I think you know a lot more about the world than I do. But I gotta tell you, from what I've seen, you want a girl who's really gonna love you, you better be her friend first and always."

Luther and I were both pleased that, coming from such different worlds, we could talk about and share something so basic. Even more important, we could laugh about our tribulations. Race and class and background started to recede as we became just two guys talking about girls, a subject that could keep us going for hours.

We talked more about our histories. I learned that when Luther was young he had picked cotton with his mother on a white man's farm, putting the cotton he picked in the sack his mother hauled. The sack was weighed at the end of the day to determine how much they were paid. Sometimes he thought the total was underweight.

I also learned that his father, Charles Mallett, had worked for the railroad and earned enough for the family to buy their small farm. They did the work of turning the soil with the use of a mule and a plow. I told Luther that my grandfather on my father's side had a farm in upstate New York, but he had a tractor to work the soil.

As we opened up to each other, I learned that Luther and Wiley had been very young, possibly seven and four years old, when his father's cousin had showed up at their home, sobbing.

"I knew something was going on, but I didn't know what it was about. My Mom and Dad talked to her and then huddled with each other. Dad told me and Wiley to ride with him. We climbed in the front seat with him and took off."

"My mind is a bit vague, but I know we drove north a long way until we turned onto a dirt road leading into the forest. What I remember is that we came to a place in the forest and got out of the car. Then I saw him, a Black man hanging by a rope tied to a tree. Dead."

Luther paused. He took a few deep breaths. "I remember that guy, his skin turned white-like, a pale color. I know his tongue was hanging out of his mouth and he had urinated all over hisself." He paused again. "I can't shake that image."

I was shocked by the story. After sitting in silence for a time I asked, "Why did this happen to him?"

"I don't know. Around here Blacks who don't want to say 'yes sir' and 'no sir' and basically just want to live their own way, they can bring destruction on their family and their selves and stuff. Your mule might get shot or your cow would die or your hog would be poisoned, it'd be something. And if you keep rebelling, you got to deal with the Klan." That could mean the end of a rope.

In the Deep South in the sixties the ultimate risk of being in the movement was death. Black people who resisted had been martyrs for generations. They were now being joined by well-known martyrs in Mississippi, including Emmett Till, Medgar Evers, Vernon Dahmer and Goodman, Chaney and Schwerner, along with many who were not as well known, such as Rev. George Lee, Mack Charles Parker and Ben Chester White, who had been murdered by the Klan in Natchez just four days after James Meredith was shot. Killing grounds were all around us. Luther and I talked and talked. We both said we were willing to face the chance of death, though we were still young, and with the brashness of young men, we thought we were invincible. We were also very scared.

What was formed sitting by the river that day was the beginning of a bond that carried us both through the summer, a bond that would be tested just three days later in Neshoba County.

Chapter 10:
Neshoba County

The phone rang early in the morning. It was the MFDP office in Jackson. We were told that on June 21 a contingent of marchers from the Meredith March would travel to the city of Philadelphia in Neshoba County to hold a memorial march for Goodman, Chaney and Schwerner. This would be the second anniversary of the day they went missing and, as we knew by 1966, the second anniversary of the day they were murdered.

Could we come to the march? Would we spread the word? It was expected that Martin Luther King, Jr. would lead the way.

That was a jolt. The idea that Martin Luther King, Jr. would be anywhere near Kosciusko was exciting. We knew that King had been in the state for a few days as one of the leaders of the Meredith March, but the March was on a route in the Delta heading toward Greenwood. We didn't expect to see the March or Rev. King anywhere on this side of the Central Hills.

The possibility that Martin Luther King, Jr. would enter Neshoba County was shocking. King would be going to perhaps the most dangerous part of the State of Mississippi, where he was seen by most of the white community as the devil incarnate. We were told that perhaps 200 people from the Meredith March would travel with him and would join local folks, gather in the small Black business section of Philadelphia known as Independence Quarters and march together to the town square, where King, Jr. would lead the memorial rally.

We all knew by then who had probably killed the three civil rights workers. Nineteen men, mostly members of the White Knights of the Ku Klux Klan, including Edgar Ray Killen, Wayne Roberts, Billy Wayne Posey, and the Imperial Wizard himself, Sam Bowers, had been indicted in 1965 for the murders. The indictments were being challenged in court. All 19 were still walking free and some were likely to be at the town square. The accused included Neshoba County Sheriff Lawrence Rainey and Deputy Sheriff Cecil Price, who were still in uniform and would be part of the police security provided for the march.

Luther and I were excited. The idea of seeing Martin Luther King, whom I had heard at the 1963 March on Washington and whom Luther had not yet had the chance to hear, was electric. For us, he was the physical embodiment of the civil rights movement. King at a march near Kosciusko? We had to be there.

Things were happening fast that month in Mississippi, a whirlwind that seemed to be funneling toward this event. Luther's brother and sister, Wiley and Jean, both teenagers, were on the Meredith March, as was my good friend Alan Moonves, from Valley Stream and Long Island CORE. We might be seeing them in Philadelphia. I felt full of energy. Gunter was more subdued in his reaction, but he got busy right away, tapping his foot on the floor as he made the first of many phone calls.

We set out to spread the word. Here was an amazing opportunity, and clearly the office in Jackson was hoping that people from counties around Neshoba could help build this one-day march into a large event. I knew that Neshoba County had a reputation for violence. I didn't yet know that Neshoba County was seen by many as a separate world, even within Mississippi. As we went house to house, and talked to people in the street or at gatherings, I began to understand.

Black people in Attala County had little reason to go to Philadelphia or anywhere else in Neshoba County. There wasn't much if anything they could get in Neshoba that couldn't be gotten in Attala. And Black people had plenty of reasons to avoid Neshoba County, notorious in Mississippi for racial violence and now notorious throughout the country for the civil rights killings. As we spread the word about the march, we encountered plenty of reluctance.

"Martin Luther King? Coming here?" asked J.E. Winters when we spoke on his porch.

"No. He's going to Philadelphia and leading a service there."

"In what church?"

"As much as I know, Mr. Winters, we're all going to gather over in the Black section of Philadelphia, the old Independence Quarters, and then march to the town square and hold a rally."

This gave most people some pause. It gave me some pause.

"Let me see if I got this right. You telling me that Martin Luther King himself is going to lead a march in the streets of Philadelphia and then put himself front and center, outside, in the downtown square?"

"That's what I'm told."

"On Tuesday?"

"Yep."

"Well, I think I need to ponder on this awhile. I may have others things I need to be doing on Tuesday."

"Well that's fine, Mr. Winters, you just let me know if there's anything you need."

Any time I got equivocation I respected it. There was no way for me to know how dangerous it would be to march in Neshoba County.

Some people were so excited about the idea of seeing Martin Luther King that they put aside their apprehensions and decided to act. We never did a count, but at least 15 to 20 people travelled from Attala County over to the march. They were mostly high school activists, like Emma Ree Rayford and Sarah Robinson, with MFDP organizers like Doc Drummond and Shirley Adams, and they traveled in small groups. Luther and I traveled in Gunter's car. I felt like this was a leap into the unknown for all of us. Later I would learn that Gunter had already been at a march in Philadelphia in April, had been arrested for possessing a weapon and was part of a legal action against the city police.

We drove separately, traveling some dirt roads and some paved, until we reached what was known as Independence Quarters. We gathered on the dirt roads near Adams Street where a collection of stores, a barbershop, a general store and an MFDP office, all linked by wooden sidewalks, shared space with a local church, the Mount Nebo Missionary Baptist Church. The church became the meeting place for the march organizers and the streets around it became the gathering place for marchers.

Perhaps 30 people had come over from the Meredith March itself, not the 200 we had anticipated. We looked around and tried to find people we knew. No one yet, but more cars were arriving. There may have been as many as 150 additional marchers from the city itself and the outlying Black community within Neshoba County.

Luther and I walked around and got in a few conversations. It didn't take long to get a picture of what was happening.

"There's a lot of white folks lining the streets to downtown. Way more than us, and they look plenty mad."

"I think there's a meeting in the church trying to figure out what to do."

"I'm not so sure we're going downtown. There's some highway patrol around, and then it's Rainey and Price and their guys and some white men they're calling auxiliary police. I don't trust 'em at all."

Luther and I walked over to the church. As we got there Rev. King came out and walked down the steps, deep in conversation with someone I did not recognize. King appeared to be taut, nervous and strained. From what we heard, the march was going to happen, but King seemed worried. I had seen him up close mostly on television and once very briefly on Long Island working with CORE, and at those times he had looked robust, calm and radiant. Now he looked gaunt.

Stokely Carmichael was also in the leadership gathered at the church, but I didn't see him. Years later he wrote that there was some discussion about whether to proceed in the face of the gathering mob, but the local activists insisted that things go forward.[5] Word soon spread that the march was going to happen. There was a network of people, probably a combination of SNCC staff and local MFDP people, who worked together as march monitors. These were people with movement experience. One young man who had a bullhorn got the attention of everyone within hearing range, and repeated a few times: "We're heading downtown. Please form up in groups. Follow the monitors."

We formed up as best as we could. There was a monitor with a bullhorn nearby. I walked with Luther among folks we did not know. Gunter was somewhere in the march with other people from Kosciusko. It was not far to the downtown square, and within a few blocks we started seeing white people. One or two of them ran ahead, perhaps to let others know we were coming.

Within six or seven blocks we started passing crowds of white folks on the sidewalks, screaming, shouting obscenities, shaking their fists and at times throwing things at us. Little clusters of Mississippi Highway Patrol officers stood around, looked at the scene and did nothing. A few seemed to smirk. Cars being driven by young white men raced their engines and roared by the marchers, sometimes swerving toward individuals or the jagged edge of the march. Within a few more blocks the white crowd began hurling firecrackers and cherry bombs at the marchers. Still, the highway patrol, the city police and the sheriff's department did nothing.

The cherry bombs were especially unnerving. They were hurled at our legs and exploded with a force that reminded me why they are called bombs. They really are small explosives and if they blew up on your leg, you went down. I saw at least three marchers fall before being picked up, and I looked at Luther with a feeling of dread. We said not a word, but for the first time we shared an immersion in the depths of fear.

Somehow we pushed on. The monitors led us in chants and song. The singing helped tremendously. All our voices joined together gave us the emotional strength to keep moving forward, one foot followed by the other, going deeper into the maelstrom. People singing as best they could:

> *Ain't gonna let no Klansman turn me round,*
> *Turn me round, turn me round,*
> *Ain't gonna let no Klansman turn me round,*
> *Gonna keep on a walkin', keep on a talkin',*
> *Marchin' on to Freedom Land.*
>
> *Ain't gonna let Sheriff Rainey turn me round,*
> *Turn me round, turn me round,*
> *Ain't gonna let Sheriff Rainey turn me round,*
> *Gonna keep on a walkin', keep on a talkin',*
> *Marchin' on to Freedom Land."*

And so on, on and on. As we marched we called out all the racists and thugs who were attacking us and added them to our song. We added "Ain't gonna let Cecil Price turn me round" and more names and "Ain't gonna let segregation turn me round." It made a difference. It gave us a collective strength that kept us heading toward the town square and the city courthouse, through the taunting and the shouting and the barrage of fireworks hurled at us by really angry white folks. At one point we passed the city jail, and the song rang out:

Ain't afraid of your jails 'cause I want my freedom
I want my freedom, I want my freedom
Ain't afraid of your jails 'cause I want my freedom
I want my freedom now.

We reached the downtown square. There were maybe two hundred of us. It looked like almost two thousand whites were packing the sidewalks and standing on the rooftops of the buildings, screaming obscenities, calling out "Niggers! You're all niggers!" Luther and I watched the rooftops constantly, looking for gunmen. Martin Luther King was in the first group to arrive at the town square and he put himself on the concrete steps in front of the county courthouse. More shouts rang out. "You're a nigger, King! Get the hell out of here!" Bottles and cans and firecrackers were thrown at him as he tried to lead a prayer. Still the local guardians of law and order did nothing.

The prayers were drowned out by the screaming mob, and Luther and I kept watching for snipers. It seemed certain someone would take a shot, try to kill Rev. King and make Neshoba County the place where he died. Somehow King remained outwardly calm, projecting a strength and a serenity which helped calm the rest of us. After the prayers were over he raised his head and looked at the crowd, the whites on the sidewalks and particularly the whites on the rooftops. He stared at them directly, and with his head held high he said in his deep baritone voice, "We are here today to commemorate the killings of Goodman, Chaney and Schwerner [this brought a little quiet] and we all know [now the white folks wanted to hear what "we" all knew] that their killers," King paused, "are standing here right now among us."

There is no transcript of the speech he gave that day, no recording or film footage, but I remember the mob going quiet when he made that challenge. They knew he was right, every last one of them, and they were so caught by surprise that they went silent. Much has been written and said about King since his death less than two years later, but on that day with that one sentence, spoken directly to the crowd and the Klansmen in their midst, he showed his character and delivered one of the most profound moments of the civil rights movement.

Then the yelling and the screaming resumed, King said a few more words I could not hear, and we started to march out of the town square.

Fire at the Freedom House

The march back was even more terrifying. In addition to the obscenities and the tossed bottles and cans and the exploding cherry bombs, there were more young white men who revved up their cars and drove very fast near the edge of the march. Now they swerved directly into the marchers, and at least one young Black man was hit and had to be taken to the hospital. The highway patrol and the white lawmen watched and did nothing.

There were people bleeding and more cars driven by white men swerving at the march, but we held together. More cherry bombs exploded. We joined hands, we sang and somehow we made it back to Independence Quarters. By the time we all reached the gathering place around Adams Street we were thirsty, tired and exhausted from the fear.

People collapsed against the wooden railings for rest. Some sat with their heads in their hands. Some were crying. We all were dazed. There were movement people ready to help us. Water was found and passed around. Wounds were tended to and bandaged. More than a few people lit cigarettes. We slowly found our way to calmness. King later said in an interview that this day was one of the most frightening days in his life.

In that setting, for the first time that day, I saw Alan Moonves, leaning against the wall of a store, dirty and disheveled, but very much Alan. He could be described as medium height, medium build, but he had one very distinguishing feature – he always had a head full of dark messy hair. He had been through the torment with us, though we had not encountered him until now.

Luther and I went over to Alan. I gave him a hug; I needed one myself. I then introduced Luther and Alan to each other and they shook hands in greeting. We all talked about what had just happened. We were shaken and weary, but none of us had been injured. We had been lucky, and we were all very relieved to be back in the relative safety of Independence Quarters.

Alan had come to the Neshoba County memorial with the small group from the Meredith March and would be heading back to join the main body of marchers near Canton that night. I was very happy to see him and Luther was suitably impressed. We gave him the address and phone number of the Freedom House in Kosciusko, not knowing then the role he would play in our lives come August.

Recruiting poster for the White Knights of the Ku Klux Klan.
By permission of the Archives Department, Mitchell Library,
Mississippi State University.

Chapter 11:
Night Riders

No one had fired a shot during that horrific day in Neshoba County. No sniper pulled the trigger, no bullet whizzed down from the rooftops.

In the late afternoon, Gunter, Luther and I drove back to Kosciusko, after the march but hours before the sun would set. We cleaned ourselves up at Mrs. Nash's, treated ourselves to dinner at the reluctantly integrated B&F Grill and relaxed on the cots at the Freedom House. We talked about the day, trying to talk through what we had seen and experienced.

None of us had ever seen such hatred spewing from a crowd, not in person. In television news reports covering the civil rights movement I had seen shorter bursts of violence, people pulled from lunch counters and beaten, or mobs in Little Rock screaming at students integrating the high school. We had seen the police attack with dogs in Birmingham, but none of us had experienced the unrestrained mob violence we had just endured.

Until that day the Meredith March had been protected by law enforcement in the state. In the days after James Meredith was shot and the March became national news, both local law enforcement and the highway patrol had protected the marchers. It makes sense this protection would break down first in Neshoba County, where moderate whites themselves felt threatened by the Klan, and local law enforcement had little interest in restraining the mob. We hadn't seen it coming.

At first that evening we had really good news, that no one from Attala County had been hurt. People had returned and news about the march had spread quickly through the community. We could not have anticipated what came next. About an hour after sunset the phone rang. Gunter took the call.

"When did it start?"

"Yeah, we can go over there right now."

"Three of us."

It had been the office in Jackson again. The Black community in Philadelphia was under assault. Groups of white gunmen had been driving through Independence Quarters, shooting into homes and businesses. Local Blacks and civil rights workers had fired back. The Jackson office was asking activists committed to armed self-defense in surrounding counties to go to their aid.

I don't think any of us hesitated. I don't remember any discussion about whether we would go back to Neshoba County. It was we just something we assumed of each other. I think the three of us shared a basic idea, that we were fully committed to the movement, that we had already put ourselves willingly in a situation where our lives were at risk every day. Here was something the movement was asking of us.

We got in the car and headed southeast on Highway 19, the state highway with no lighting that ran all the way to Meridian. We drove into Neshoba County in the dark in a car with unconcealed weapons. A rifle, two revolvers and one small Beretta pistol were openly displayed on the back shelf and on the seats.

The countryside was flat, and Highway 19 was taking us there on a paved road. There was only a sliver of moonlight and it barely cast a shadowy illumination on the meadows and trees on both sides of the road. Gunter drove below the speed limit as Luther and I watched for cars following us or coming at us from side roads. At one point we saw the faint glow of blinking lights in front of us. As we got closer we could see that the road was blocked. A police car with top lights flashing was blocking the southbound lane we were traveling on, and a second, unmarked car was parked at an angle across both lanes. Gunter brought the car to a stop.

Two white men stood on the roadway, one a large man in uniform, the other, an older, grizzled fellow, dressed in slacks with a starched white short-sleeve shirt. He had a holster and gun hanging from his belt. He might have had a badge pinned to his shirt. He leaned against the car and watched us as the man in uniform came to the window.

"Could be Sheriff Rainey," whispered Gunter without moving his lips.

"Where you boys think you're goin'?" the man in uniform said as he looked at us and the car.

"Philadelphia."

"No you ain't. Road's closed. You just turn yourselves 'round and get the hell out 'a here. You hear me?" A long hard stare.

Gunter nodded, backed up, turned the car around and headed back north. I was silent with shock, turning around to see if we were being followed. Nothing. Luther broke the silence.

"Hey Gunter, where are we goin' now?"

"That was something. The bastards. Just want to keep us out. Just protecting the attackers. Someone I know can lead us in."

Soon he turned onto a dirt road and brought us to a house on the edge of the woods. We all got out. A chance to stretch, a chance to breathe. I don't remember saying anything, but I was at a heightened level of alertness as I came to terms with the danger we were facing. Gunter got involved in a conversation with the man who was at the house, a Black man older than us. I never learned his name.

"Okay, he's going to take us in."

Gunter took the rifle and one of the revolvers, Luther took the other revolver, leaving me with the Beretta, which was fine with me. I wasn't much good with any of the handguns and at least the Beretta was small and easy to carry. It fit in the pocket of my pants. In a misguided attempt to keep my left hand from getting snagged, I took off my wristwatch and put it in my shirt pocket.

Gunter's contact led us on a footpath through the woods. We walked as briskly as the trail allowed until our guide turned and said, "Someone's behind us." We were still among the trees. Within seconds a shot rang out. We started to run. I never saw who fired at us or who was chasing us. I just ran as fast as I could over this unknown terrain without tripping, my entire focus being to flee as fast as possible.

At one point we had to climb over a half-rotten jagged fence. As I fumbled over the top, the watch fell out of my pocket. Even though we never heard a second shot there was no way I was pausing in my flight. The watch, a high school graduation gift from my parents, was inscribed at my request with the words, "Eternal vigilance is the price of liberty." It may still be buried somewhere in the pine forest of Neshoba County.

I don't know if we ran for 45 seconds or 5 minutes, moving through time as if I were dreaming, scrambling and stumbling and trying to run. Tree branches slapped my face, bits of nature cracked under my shoes until, after running forever, we were suddenly in a clearing in the back of the stores of Independence Quarter. There was no longer anyone chasing us.

Somehow we got some water, and Gunter went to find someone who was in charge. My mind was racing with images of what had just happened, as if it were all on a reel of film that I could examine frame by frame. I heard the shot over and over again. The more I thought about it, the more it became engraved in my memory. It became a chase which would revisit me as a nightmare for years.

Soon we were directed to a wooden ladder that took us up to the roof of a one-story building overlooking two dirt roads of Independence Quarter. I could see the area where we had gathered that afternoon. Now it was empty, a possible route for cars with white men ready to shoot at us. We were on the rooftops, a scattering of men everywhere, mostly Black, all armed. There were no women in sight. I settled in next to Luther as we waited and watched.

We were told there had been three waves of attacks already. Each one had been met with return fire. The wooden sidewalks in front of the shops were covered with shattered glass from broken windows. The third attack had been from some distance rather than from cars on the roads below. No one in the Black community had been shot, but people thought one of the attackers might have been hit. It was much quieter now, and I certainly felt calmer on the roof than I had felt when we been racing through the woods.

We were on the roof for a very long time. It had a slight angle to it, but the best part was the false front, a short wall of wood that looked like a design feature at street level but worked as a barricade for those of us on the roof. By moving along the roof top while crouched behind this wall, I could keep my head low and still keep an eye on the street.

Suddenly a car appeared a few blocks away. It was on a road approaching us and whoever was driving was driving fast. Everyone on the rooftops was on high alert. I could feel tightness in my shoulders and in my stomach. The car kept coming, and someone in the back seat quickly stuck a gun barrel out the window and started shooting at us. Instantly there was a return volley from the rooftops. I contributed to the volume of fire with one shot from the Beretta. The car spun around and raced away.

A few people on the roof took parting shots at the car. It felt empowering to be part of an integrated group of relative strangers able to stand together against the night riders. The seductive thrill of combat also tugged at me, made easier by the fact that no one got hurt.

After perhaps another half an hour, a single car drove slowly into Independence Quarters and stopped. A young Black man in a police uniform got out. I had no idea what was happening. I had not until this moment ever seen a Black police officer in Mississippi. Many men on the rooftops apparently knew this man and started taunting him. "Hey Tripp, you motherfucker, what are you doing here? Rainey send you over to get yourself killed?" There followed an exchange of cursing and yelling. Tripp seemed to be telling people to disarm, orders – if they were orders – that were met with hoots and more insults. After a few minutes he got back in his car and drove away.

Tripp, I later learned, was the nickname for Willie Windham, a young Neshoba County Black man willing to police the Black community and beat and ultimately kill at the behest of the white supremacists running law enforcement in Philadelphia. He was in uniform from June of 1965 to December of 1966, when he was driven out of the county by the Black community after some particularly brutal act.

We stayed on the roof for another hour or so after that confrontation, and all was quiet. Finally, a local organizer, someone I did not know but who was clearly in charge, came around to folks on the rooftops and said it was over. "Put your guns away," he told us. It was easy to comply. I was more than ready to be done.

We climbed down the ladder, glad for the chance to be out of the line of fire. People were gathering around in small clusters. I didn't see anyone I knew besides Luther, who I was next to most of the night, and Gunter, but at one point I did find myself in a group near James Letherer, known as the one-legged marcher, made famous for his tenacity during the Selma to Montgomery March in 1965. He was still venting. "They shot right at me," he was saying bitterly, "and all I could do was throw my crutch at them."

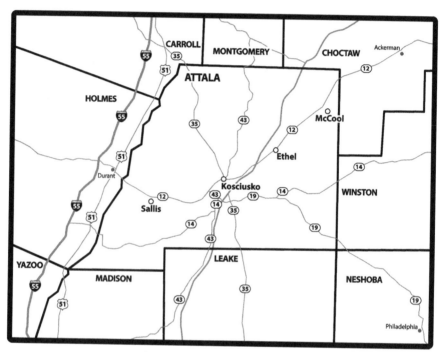

Map of Attala County and surrounding area.

Fire at the Freedom House

Chapter 12:
Try Again

We slept in the MFDP office in Independence Quarters after the shooting was over. Folks took turns staying up on guard duty, but by now the local community had enough people available to protect the entire neighborhood, and Luther and Gunter and I were able to take a break. Exhausted, I simply slept on a blanket on the floor. We awoke to some coffee and corn bread and the news that the Meredith Marchers were talking about a second march in Neshoba County in two days, on Friday. We returned to Kosciusko that Wednesday morning, June 22.

That day we surrendered to the sun and the heat. Luther went back home to check on his mom and probably to visit a girlfriend. Gunter and I relaxed at the Freedom House. It was a day of rest. I wrote some letters. Gunter made some phone calls, first to Kosciusko folks who had been on the march. A few people just came on by. Emma Ree Rayford and Shirley Yowk stopped over. Both were students at Tipton High who had been active in the movement. Emma Ree Rayford was solid and carried herself in a way that commanded respect, while Shirley Yowk was full of humor and smart talk. Both had an inner strength that propelled them into the movement.

Police Chief Harvey arrived and parked his police car on the road in front of the Freedom House. Gunter went outside and stood talking with him for some time. I realized by now that his visits were routine. His demeanor was calm and professional. He was a welcome contrast to Lawrence Rainey and Cecil Price and what we had just seen of law enforcement in Neshoba County. Of course, Chief Harvey could still arrest us whenever it suited him.

We learned on the news that police in Canton had gassed and beaten participants in the Meredith March. The pretext for the use of force was that the marchers did not have a permit to set up tents in the local park.

Using tear gas and clubs, police and highway patrol had torn down the tents and beaten the marchers. Any pretense of protecting the marchers was gone.

We knew Alan had planned to return to Canton from Neshoba County. Though we had not heard from Luther's siblings, Wiley and Jean, we had every reason to believe that they had been with the group that had tried to set up tents in the park. There was plenty of reason to worry. We had no way to contact them.

Their mother, Lenora Mallet, had lived through a week when three of her children had been at risk of violent harm participating in the civil rights movement. My own parents now called the Freedom House regularly. I did my best to assure them that I was fine and that everything was alright, but all I really conveyed was that I would remain in Mississippi. There was no way I could convince them that I would be fine in the days ahead, since I could not be sure myself what might happen next.

On Thursday we received another call from the Jackson office. They confirmed that the attacks on Tuesday had become national news, and the leaders of the Meredith March, in agreement with the Neshoba County MFDP, had decided to return to Philadelphia for a Second Memorial March for Goodman, Chaney and Schwerner the following day, on Friday, June 24.

We spread the word, but folks already knew what had happened on Tuesday, and there was reluctance to return to Neshoba County. The people from the Attala County movement who had gone to the first march told their neighbors a sobering story, and word spread quickly. The decision to go on Friday was a difficult one, though a few people came for the second time. Given a new chance to hear Martin Luther King, as many as ten new folks, mostly young people, decided to take the risk. It was impossible to know what would happen on a second march. Behind the scenes, Mississippi Gov. Paul Johnson contacted city and county officials in Neshoba and made it clear that he did not want the march on Friday to bring more negative publicity to the state.

This time there was much more of a presence of news media, both print and television. When we arrived in Independence Quarters we found perhaps 300 people ready to march, not a huge increase from Tuesday, but this time dozens of reporters and cameramen gathered in clusters around cars and vans parked on the dirt roads. I recognized Murray Kempton from the *New York Post* - not that I knew him personally, but I recognized him from the photograph that ran with his column. In 1966 the *New York Post* was a home for serious journalism and Murray Kempton was a respected columnist. In addition, there were Mississippi Highway Patrol officers on their best behavior, actually blocking any cars approaching the march from the white section of town.

We arrived while there was a service being conducted at the Mount Nebo Baptist Church. Soon after it was over we started our march to the town square. This was the one time I saw Stokely Carmichael close up. He was radiant with energy. Though this was not the Delta, where he had felt at home as an organizer, and though Neshoba was instead what he later described as scrubby hills and swampy bottoms infested with mosquitoes and the Klan, he looked like he fit right in, like he was a force of nature.[6]

Our mood regarding the march was cautious. We formed up again, following the directions of march monitors. We found the media covering us as soon as we started to walk along the road, making it feel to me like the media itself became part of the march. Any notion that the media alone could keep things peaceful was misplaced. Within a few blocks we again found the sidewalks packed with hostile white folks, some of whom were again shouting and calling us "niggers" and "nigger-lovers." This time, however, there were highway patrol officers separating the angry crowd from us, and no cherry bombs were hurled, no cars driven at the line of marchers.

We sang again to expel our fears, and this time we found our collective voice more easily, singing loud enough to drown out the white people yelling at us. We were led by the march monitors in songs which were a bit less strident than the ones we had needed on Tuesday. These songs were more calming, though they were just as resolute:

> *Woke up this morning with my mind*
> *Stayed on freedom*
> *Woke up this morning with my mind*
> *Stayed on freedom*
> *Hallelu, Hallelu, Hallelujah.*
> *Walkin' and talkin' with my mind*

Stayed on freedom
Walkin' and talkin' with my mind
Stayed on freedom
Hallelu, Hallelu, Hallelujah.

And

Paul and Silas bound in jail,
Had no money for to go their bail.
Keep your eyes on the prize,
Hold on, my Lordy, hold on.
Hold on,
Hold on,
Keep your eyes on the prize,
Hold on.

The singing and the words of the songs let us hold on to each other emotionally as we walked that gauntlet of anger yet again.

The downtown square was packed with an even larger crowd of white folks, many of them now quiet spectators but some of them screaming and yelling insults. Some white people tried to throw things at us, bottles and cans and all kinds of garbage, but they were kept at a distance by law enforcement at every level. We were a small group in a sea of hostility, but powerful forces within the local white community did not want this to become a national news story and another major embarrassment. This time the event was being recorded and photographed.

Yet when a local Black preacher, Rev. Collier, attempted to lead a prayer, he was shouted down by a section of the crowd on the sidewalk. Stokely Carmichael addressed himself to those of us on the march, saying, "The people gathered around us represent America in its truest form. They represent a sick and resisting society that sits in the United Nations and gives lip service to democracy." Rev. King tried to speak to everyone there, marchers and the hostile crowd. Before he spoke, both Luther and I had moved among the marchers and I could not make out his words. Later I was told he was more conciliatory and inclusive than Stokely, but these different approaches seemed to make no difference to those who jeered both men with cries of "You're a nigger" and "Get the hell out of here, nigger."

It was not a day of reconciliation.

Our safe return march to the street corners in Independence Quarters felt like a victory for all of us. On this day, we could feel our power.

Button for the Meredith March,
sold at the final rally in Jackson.
Courtesy of Jo Freeman

Chapter 13:
Return of the Meredith Marchers

Two days after the second march in Neshoba County, the Meredith March was to arrive in Jackson and hold its final rally.

Luther went alone in his family truck to pick up his siblings and finally learned what had happened to them.

Jean and Wiley had joined the Meredith March before Greenwood and had been with the group as it marched south through the Mississippi Delta, over 7,000 square miles of deep, rich alluvial soil perfect for growing cotton, on to Itta Bena and Yazoo City. At Yazoo City the Meredith March went southeast on Highway 16 on the way toward Jackson. They stopped for the night in Canton.

Everything changed in Canton. When the marchers tried to set up camp for the night, they were ordered to disperse by the Mississippi Highway Patrol. Wiley and Jean were trying to set up tents when tear gas was fired and state troopers kicked and beat people until the area was cleared. After Jean had been knocked to the ground, a state trooper stood over her and pointed a bayonet directly at her throat. She was able to roll away from him in the chaos. She spent that night protected by a local family.

Luther brought them both home, to the great relief of their mother. She was proud of her children's involvement in the movement and encouraged them all to remain active. "I'd be out there myself if I was young," she said. But as Luther told me later, his mother had been worried sick. She did not hide her joy at the safe return of Jean and Wiley,

Gunter and I went to Jackson in the project car to pick up Betty Jones, who had been in Vicksburg and had joined the last section of the Meredith March. We arrived downtown to find police barricades and blocked streets. Somehow we found a place to park the car and walked to the edge of the crowd, estimated at 15,000, just as the rally at the state capital was ending. The state capitol building was still ringed by armed white men. Since the rally was over, we walked the full circle around the building looking for Betty.

The building was ringed by three official groups of white men in uniform. As we walked around the full circle, the contrast was compelling. We first passed National Guard troops called up by the governor, uniformed men in sharp military formation holding M-1 rifles. Next we passed Mississippi Highway Patrol officers in uniform, looking professional and keeping some semblance of order. The third group was a collection of local police and some rangers from the Fish and Game Department, holding gas masks, some standing in formation, others lounging on the grass. Frankly, many of them looked like thugs. One of them, leaning back on the lawn, flicked his middle finger at us.

We didn't find Betty in the crowd, but I simply followed Gunter's lead and we were taken home by an older Black woman who approached us and spoke to Gunter. She may have known him from an earlier time. She took us to her apartment and put out food for dinner. There was a knock on the door and in strode a tall Black woman in her twenties, her head held high, with a stately bearing and piercing eyes. She gave Gunter a long hug. I was introduced to Betty Jones.

While we all ate dinner Betty filled us in on the end of the march. "I thought I was coming to the end of James Meredith's march, but it didn't seem like his anymore," she said. "Seemed liked a march of the entire Jackson Black community. People poured out of their houses to join us. There were so many people it looked like the streets were filled forever. I saw a few scuffles, and the usual nonsense from white folks who still love the Confederacy, but there was an amazing group of speakers at the end."

She paused as we finished dinner. "Meredith was there and spoke, and so was Lawrence Guyot and other MFDP folks and some doctor, something like Pussant, who was really good. And I got to hear Martin Luther King himself, right here in Jackson. It really made me feel like there's no holding back this change that's coming."

The three of us left together in the dark, driving the Natchez Trace back to the Freedom House. The return of Betty Jones to Kosciusko was good for everyone. She was a match for Gunter in every way. She had arrived with him in Kosciusko, the first civil rights workers to

Fire at the Freedom House

settle in Attala County. With her Black Mississippi accent and her outgoing personality, she fit in well with the local community and made friends easily.

Staying in the Freedom House with Gunter, Betty brought some order and cleanliness to a space where there had been only male energy for weeks. Betty and Gunter shared the back room, and while it did have a door, it was clearly time for me to stay somewhere else. The next day it was arranged for me to stay at the home of Elmore and Beatrice Winfrey.

Bumper sticker created by the
Attala County MFDP in the summer of 1966.

Chapter 14:
Settling In

Mr. and Mrs. Winfrey were early pioneers of the civil rights movement in Attala County. They had housed Betty and Gunter when they first came to town in the fall of 1965, a bold act which placed them at considerable risk. The homes of Black people who provided housing to civil rights workers throughout the state were often attacked with gunfire and at times with arson and bombs. Now Elmore and Beatrice Winfrey were choosing to house me and face those risks again.

The first night I was at their home on North Natchez Street we chatted briefly before I was shown by Mrs. Winfrey to a large room with a comfortable double bed. "Make yourself at home," Mrs. Winfrey said, as she also gave me directions to the bathroom. This is a delight, I thought to myself. I slept that night floating on feathers.

It was a shock early the next morning when I found that Mr. and Mrs. Winfrey had spent the night sleeping on the living room couch. They had given up their bedroom in order to make me comfortable. As much as I appreciated their hospitality, I could not possibly accept their room.

Mrs. Winfrey made me breakfast, and when we sat down to eat, I had to bring up the subject.

"Ah, thank you very much." I started. "You know I really appreciate you putting me up, but I couldn't help but notice that you and Mr. Winfrey slept on the couch last night."

"Well son, you looked mighty worn down when you got here, and we wanted you to get a good sleep."

"Yes, and I certainly did, but I can't be putting you out of your own bedroom. Could I please sleep on the couch in the future?"

They moved me to the couch that night, and I think we were all more comfortable.

Gunter picked me up after breakfast. We hardly talked in the car, though he did ask how things went and I told him about the bedroom but that things were now fine. He dropped me off at the Freedom House, then went on to something else. That's the way it was with Gunter. I often did not know where he was going when he drove away.

Gunter's departure left me alone with Betty for the first time. We sat on the front porch, Betty on a hard wooden chair that was propped against the wooden frame of the window, me with my back leaning against the side of the house. It was quiet and hot. We both watched the street.

Betty got right to the point. "Where are you from?" she asked.

I told her about New York and Oberlin and my Italian background. She asked about the neighborhoods I lived in, what my parents did and what my schools were like. She didn't seem to care about the Italian part, I think because the bottom line was color – I was white.

"You ever been in jail?"

"Nope, not yet. I can't say I'm eager for the experience." I told her about the work I had done with the movement before coming to Mississippi and about Long Island CORE. That struck a nerve.

"I thought of myself as CORE at one time," Betty told me, "but I've seen so many groups and names come and go in the past few years that mostly I just think of us as civil rights workers. Believe me, you can get a headache with some of these meetings. Did you see the leaflet for the Black-Out? We signed that as civil rights workers," Betty said, making her point clear to me.

I had seen the leaflet when our group was there in the winter. Distributed in December of 1965, it had the title "Black-Out." The effort was statewide and was an attempt by the MFDP to put white-owned businesses on notice. It did not use the word "boycott", I think because of some legal advice from Jackson, but it asked the community to decide not to shop at ten stores, including both Sunflower Markets in Kosciusko. The leaflet read:

BLACK – OUT
This means we are asking all Negroes not to buy at the stores listed below until they hire some Negroes at good jobs. Such as salesladies and cashiers at regular pay, not just jobs sweeping the floor or delivering packages or working in the stock room at low pay. We have asked all managers

or owners of the stores listed below to hire Negroes as salesladies or cashiers and they have not done so.

So don't buy at these stores until Negroes are hired:
1. Fred's Dollar Store
2. Ben Franklin Five and Dime Store
3. J.C. Penney's
4. Morgan and Lindsey
5. Shainberg's
6. Sears and Roebuck
7. W.C. Leonard and Leonard's Bargain Basement
8. Sunflower Super Market #10
9. Sunflower Super Market #11
10. Bradley's Super Market

Nothing will happen to you if you want to go into one of these stores, but please don't because by staying out you are helping yourselves. Stay out even if you have a credit card. It may mean no Christmas presents but explain to your children and relatives why you are doing this. The Black Out will begin Monday, December 20.

You can buy at any other stores that aren't listed on this leaflet. The Negro community must stand together and show them we mean business.

FREEDOM NOW
Betty Jones and Gunter Frentz
Civil Rights Workers

The Black Out had fizzled in Kosciusko, Betty said. They hadn't done enough community work and there wasn't enough support for it, but "it served notice me and Gunter meant to be a force to be reckoned with."

This gave me a chance to ask my own question.

"How did you start working with Gunter?"

"I joined CORE in Vicksburg and came down here to work with a Head Start group called CDGM. Gunter was there already. He'd left some boring job in New York and we got together doing Head Start work. Then we thought we could do more, and CORE sent us here."

"Gunter's from New York?"

Betty laughed. "Matt, you don't know a thing about Gunter, do you?"

"Well, he doesn't exactly talk much."

"I'll give you that," she replied. "Look, Gunter came here from New York but he wasn't born there. He went to New York from Germany with just his mom after the war, and I think his dad was in the Nazi army. That's all he wants to tell me. That's some powerful stuff. Maybe he's trying to get rid of a lot of ghosts."

I had met some British activists with the health care workers in Jackson, but this was the first I heard about anyone with Gunter's background. While there was still much that I did not understand, at least now I had some insight into Gunter.

Betty went on, "Gunter's really good about getting things done. It was Gunter who found the Winfreys, I think through someone in Meridian, and without them we never could have gotten started here. The thing about Gunter is you can trust him when he puts his life on the line."

As we talked that morning, Betty described a larger vision of what she and Gunter were trying to do. "This is a small community where people know each other and people talk. We don't come attached to any of the old divisions people have here, personal or religious or whatever. We say strength is in numbers, and that means everybody." Betty and Gunter were able to initiate civil rights meetings at both Baptist and Methodist churches and work with anybody ready to step forward.

Our conversation ended abruptly when Gunter returned, bringing both Luther and Wiley Mallett. This would my first introduction to Wiley. What I remember is meeting a very warm guy, dressed casually in jeans and a shirt, who spoke with self-confidence.

Wiley could put a turn on a phrase that would make you remember a point. He was just returning from a march through what local white politicians called "the sovereign state of Mississippi" and he could say, "Sovereign? Don't they realize they gave that up at Appomattox?"

Wiley said he was full of energy from his participation in the civil rights movement and wanted to do what he could during the summer months.

In the first weeks after the Meredith March, Luther and I methodically visited every gas station in Kosciusko and the surrounding area to check out whether or not they had integrated their bathrooms. Most days Wiley joined us. The best location for a gas station is where there is traffic, and in Kosciusko that meant Highway 35 and the much-traveled Highway

12, which made these local gas stations part of interstate commerce. That meant they were prohibited from having segregated bathrooms.

Ah, but they did have them. So we drove around to the gas stations to probe exactly what they were doing when people asked to use the bathroom. At one station with only two restrooms the owner simply refused to allow Luther to use either one. "We don't have no bathrooms," the owner said to Luther's face. Most of the gas stations had three restrooms, two for whites labeled "White Ladies" or "White Men" and one in the back labeled "Colored." The separate bathrooms for Black people were never equal. They were always dirty, sometimes filthy, were rarely stocked with supplies and often had no toilet seat.

At one station when I asked for a bathroom, I was sent to the one in the rear. This was not an uncommon experience for white civil rights workers, since we were considered by many whites to be race traitors. The rear bathroom at this station was filthy, and I wanted to see whether the bathroom for white men was any better, so I went back to the white attendant, a man in his forties with a grizzled face, and said there was no toilet paper, could I use a different bathroom? "Hell, no." he said. "That's what you come in here for. You can get smart if you want to, but you're not gonna use the other one."

I was irked, but at least there was no violence. Of course he knew what I had come in there for. Gas station owners were talking about us by then and I revealed myself to be a Yankee as soon as I said one sentence, or sometimes even one word. ("I knowed who you was as soon's you said 'Howdy'" was a comment I had heard from one gas station owner.) I went back to the car and wrote notes detailing what had happened. At some point we would submit formal complaints to the Department of Justice.

We also took notice of what we were charged for food, though I can't say much for our food choices. The three of us stopped at The Mug on Highway 35, and Luther went to get three vanilla milkshakes. The posted price was 30 cents each, but he was charged $1.56 by the white man at the counter. Twenty minutes later, I went to the counter, ordered three vanilla milkshakes and was charged 94 cents. When I asked why Luther had been charged more, the icy reply was, "Our prices are subject to change without notice."

Wiley continued to work with the movement through the entire summer. Though he was not active every day, Wiley was there for every action and much of the day-to-day work. He taught me about the reality of being Black in Attala County and dealing with the white community. He told me which white men had fathered children with Black women who worked for them or whom they could control, and how a white man had once told Wiley to fetch his older sister, Leila Mae, for the man. Wiley had refused and had warned his parents. The white man backed off.

He also told me about the lynched body he and Luther had seen with their father, the same horror I had heard about from Luther, though Wiley remembered the man as being the husband of a cousin in the family. Wiley was haunted by the same image that haunted Luther, the man's body swinging from the limb of a gum tree "with his tongue hanging out." He could still visualize the experience, and he said he recalled that the lynched man was hanged with a cotton ply rope.

At the same time it was Wiley who was the first to mention to me the names of good white folk, like Dr. Willard Barnes who treated Black patients with fairness and dignity, and a local farmer who would sit at the table with the Malletts, but only when he was confident that he would not be seen by other whites. I hadn't yet encountered helpful white people, though later I did throughout Attala County, like the attorney Aaron Condon and a white truck driver who often drove routes up north. I continued to hear other stories about white people in the county who crossed the color line in positive ways, but the contact was always discreet.

I gradually met the Mallett family. Their sister Jean, who was as strong as Luther and Wiley, was part of every major civil rights activity in the county, was active in the day to day work and was arrested with a large group of us later in the summer. In the first weeks after the Meredith March she was needed at home. The expectation was that Jean, as the only other female in the house, would be the person helping her mother. There were farm chores to be done, housework to be done, and the youngest sibling, ten-year-old Jerry, still needed to be watched. It was also a good time for her to have a pause.

There never was much of a pause though, because Jean felt that you couldn't be in the movement one day and not in the movement the next. She had already learned about the risk of being a Black female in

Fire at the Freedom House

a white power society, she knew about the power of white men and she was not going to live under that fear. That was a huge part of her drive. She remembered a time as a young child when her mother was picking butter beans for pay. A white farmer took Jean out to where her mother was working and Jean remembers him saying they ought to stay together, because he couldn't be responsible for what some of these white boys might do. "Children grow up fast around here, you know what I mean?" she remarked to me.

Jean had already grown up a great deal by the time she participated in the Meredith March. The March had registered thousands of new voters as it traveled through the Delta to Jackson, but in the national media the March was a one-note story, and that story was the use of the words "Black Power" by SNCC activists. Jean told me later that she had returned from the March embracing the slogan, but its meaning wasn't clear.

Did Black Power mean the end of nonviolence? If so, we were already practicing self-defense in Attala County. Was the slogan focused on counties with a majority of Black voters? If so, it gave little guidance in the Central Hills, where white people were in the majority. Did it mean the exclusion of white people as organizers? Both Fannie Lou Hamer and Lawrence Guyot, early SNCC members now in leadership in the MFDP, supported self-defense but disagreed with the exclusion of whites as organizers.

Ultimately, I think people came to understand the slogan Black Power as meaning power to the powerless. Black Power was the alternative to the existing system, which placed all power in the hands of white folk. Black Power called for power to those who had first endured slavery and then had lived with power taken away from them.

But at that time, when the slogan was first articulated during the Meredith March, the call for Black Power stirred great conflict within the civil rights movement. Some organizations feared a white backlash, both political and financial.

Partly because Attala County had not drawn the attention of national organizations, there was no history of competing civil rights groups in Kosciusko, and the struggles within and between those organizations were a distant rumble. The MFDP in the county was autonomous within the civil rights movement, nurtured and guided by Black leadership in Jackson. In Attala County in 1966, local Black activists continued to welcome our integrated group into their homes and into their circle of trust.

Most nights after I had been out canvassing with Luther, I stayed with Beatrice and Elmore Winfrey. One night I stayed on the Mallett farm. Luther's mother told him to be sure to bring me home for dinner and there simply was no question about it. Since her eldest son was risking his life with me on a daily basis, and Jean and Wiley were committed to remaining actively involved, Lenora Mallett wanted to get a close look at this white Northerner who was back in the county after the shooting in February.

The Malletts lived on a farm on the northern outskirts of Kosciusko, off a dirt road that led to other land owned by Black families. The area was separated from white farmers by only a few miles, and it was rumored that the Klan held meetings in a barn on one of those farms. We drove through fields planted with a mix of cotton, yams, butter beans and other crops to a dusty wooden farmhouse with chickens in the yard and pigs in a nearby pen. Wiley met us at the door and led us inside.

The house was modest and immaculate. Luther introduced me.

"Mom, this is Matt."

"I'm very glad to meet you, Mrs. Mallett."

"Well now," she responded, "I've been hearing quite a bit about you. How are you liking your time in Miss'ippi?"

"So far we seem to be doing fine," was all I could say. "You have some very brave children. I'm happy to be here to see things change."

"You been around colored folks much?" No mincing words here.

"Yes, ma'am. I worked in the civil rights movement up North, and more than a few Black people urged me to come South."

"Well, you can't get more South than Miss'ippi. We're pretty hungry. You like collard greens?"

We had dinner at the big wooden family table in the dining room. Wiley and Jean brought in the food while Mrs. Mallett peppered me with questions about my family background, my college experience and my time in Kosciusko. Luther sat back and took it all in. Dinner was fried chicken, buttered yams and the promised collard greens, all served with cornbread and tea. Once we started eating, the conversation slowed and became more casual. Dessert was apple pie served in big chunks. We had no problem eating our fill.

I thought Luther would be driving me back to town, but Mrs. Mallett had us sit together and talk for the next few hours. I think she learned more about me than any adult in Attala County. I became comfortable with her, but I was surprised when she told Luther that he needed to do some farm work in the morning and that I could stay over in his room. I gave Luther a quick glance, and he gave me one slight nod of his head. I was staying the night.

It was a bit of a shock when we retired to Luther's room. One bed. I'd never slept on the same mattress with a guy before, and I am certain that Luther had never imagined he would share his bed with a white guy. We were tentative as we got into the bed together. Luther muttered, "I'm not working in no cotton field tomorrow," before we said goodnight. We were exhausted and despite the awkwardness of the moment we both fell asleep easily.

Luther was up early. I woke to the smell of frying eggs and emerged to find a serious Mrs. Mallett cooking breakfast and engaged in a quiet but intense conversation with Luther. This must have been about the farm work, and I was secretly hoping that Luther would win. I hadn't yet done any serious physical labor in my life and I had soft hands. I didn't want to spend a hot day working in the fields. It was not up to me, but my real concern was that I would be so inept that I would look foolish.

Somehow Luther won out. The issue had come down to cotton. He told me later that he had made a promise to himself a few years ago never to work in the cotton fields again. It wasn't time for planting or harvesting, so the task might have been weeding, but it didn't matter. He was not working in the cotton fields of Mississippi, period. A taciturn Mrs. Mallett served us breakfast and packed us some food. We took off for another day of canvassing.

Before Luther and I left, Jean found a moment to speak with me. "Mom thinks you're a pretty solid guy," she said quietly. "Not bad for a white boy."

With the return of the Meredith Marchers, and the absence of any rancor or splits, the movement in Attala County was ready to surge.

CIVIL RIGHTS MEETING
PLACE: WESLEY METHODIST CHURCH
DATE: THURSDAY, JULY 14th
TIME: 8:00 P.M.
LET'S TALK ABOUT THE MARCH
LET'S ELECT A FREEDOM DEMOCRATIC
    COMMITTEE
GUEST SPEAKER: MR. LAWRENCE GUYOT
    HEAD OF THE FREEDOM DEMOCRATIC PARTY
COME TO THE MEETING
FREEDOM NOW

MFDP leaflet, Kosciusko, July 1966.

Fire at the Freedom House

Chapter 15:
Ballots and Booze

We now had the largest concentration of organizers and activists the county had ever seen.

The main organizers were the four of us who worked out of the Freedom House - Betty, Gunter, Luther and me - all of us committed full-time to building the civil rights movement. We had given ourselves to the work. We knew that we might ultimately flee the county, unless we were jailed or killed first. Three of us had no local roots and were not at risk of losing jobs, homes or land. Luther was putting everything at risk.

The people I am calling activists were men and women of all ages who were rooted in the community and who were building the movement. The activists, adults and an expanding group of high school students, were concentrated in Kosciusko. Some participated in a meeting or a march, some took part in almost everything, from voter registration work to the attempt to integrate the restaurants, the movie theater and all public places. The adult activists were risking their jobs, their homes, and sometimes their land. The students were risking their futures. They were all risking their lives. Together, as our numbers grew, we began to feel stronger. Our energy felt boundless. We were full of optimism.

The adults who formed the core of the MFDP were drawn from all economic levels in the Black community. Sharecroppers who farmed for white landowners were beholden to the landowner for both work and a place to live. They had more to lose if they became activists. Black farmers who owned their farms were more self-sufficient and often more ready to take risks. Many farm laborers worked as hired hands, picking crops like peas and cotton at harvest time. Some people had no jobs at all. A small group of Black people in the community were professionals, teachers and administrators and city employees. There were Black businesses selling to the Black community. Some small businesses, like the barbershops and the auto shop, provided significant resources to the movement. Alan Kern's Deluxe Barber Shop on South Jackson helped with bail money when people started getting arrested.

The central focus was always registering people to vote. The leaders of the local MFDP, including Dock Drummond, J.P. Presley and Susie Bell, were determined to reach every Black household with the message that the poll tax and the literacy test were gone. The Voting Rights Act of 1965 and the 24th Amendment prohibiting the poll tax were victories we built on. It was important that every qualified Black resident be registered. The requirements were U.S. citizenship, 21 years of age, no felony convictions, two years of residency in Mississippi and one year of residency in Attala County. An exception was granted "for a minister of the gospel in charge of an organized church and his wife," who could register to vote after six months of residency.

Dock Drummond, who had been building the local movement since the arrival of Betty and Gunter, had decided to run for the congressional seat in District One as an MFDP candidate, a step which made him a luminous target for the local Klan. "How can you put yourself out there like that?" I had to ask him.

"Someone's got to do it," was all he said.

We were given an unexpected gift when, on July 1, the Mississippi Local Option Law went into effect. Until that time, the entire state had lived under alcohol prohibition. Now the Local Option Law allowed each county to hold an election, subject to state rules, to remain "dry" or to go "wet," which would allow the manufacture, possession and sale of "intoxicating liquors." This was known in the state as "the whiskey vote," beer being subject to other regulations. Petitions were quickly signed and gathered in the white community to put the entire issue of both beer and hard alcohol on the ballot in Attala County in early August.

No other issue had divided the local white community so deeply in the twentieth century. The governor of the state urged an honest look at what he called "backdoor drinking habits" in the state, his own included, and the reality of taxes. The truth was that alcohol was being consumed everywhere, with moonshine the liquor of choice in rural communities, and smuggled bottles of fine whiskey available, particularly in the cities, to anyone able and willing to pay. Smuggling was an epidemic. Since folks were already drinking, the argument went, it was high time for government to collect its fair share of taxes.

In Attala County, more than a few people wanted to sip their whiskey on the front porch, in peace, rather than sneak it into the house through the back door. Some simply wanted to keep business dollars in the county, since it was expected that at least one of the neighboring counties would go wet. And some were eager to break the power of the bootleggers, who ran illicit stills and might be paying the county sheriff to look the other way.

The bootleggers, both white and Black, in a rare show of racial unity, wanted Attala County to stay dry. This was their business, and their livelihood was at stake. They were joined by those who genuinely believed in prohibition, who believed that alcohol brought crime and debauchery, and they had some statistics in their favor. Sheriff Malone appeared to stay neutral, but anyone making money from moonshine wanted the county to remain dry. On this issue, those who wanted to put the bootleggers in jail joined with the bootleggers to urge a vote for continued prohibition.

Attala County was over 60 percent white, and registered whites far outnumbered registered Blacks. But with the white vote deeply divided and hotly contested, suddenly the prospect of hundreds of Black voters had real weight. How would Black people vote on this issue? The Black community itself was divided in many ways along the same lines as the white community. Some had ethical or religious beliefs that discouraged the use of alcohol, while many others drank the corn whisky of the Black bootlegger. What could the white community do to influence the Black vote?

At this important moment the local MFDP made the perfect choice. It took no side at all. "Wet or dry, register to vote." This call challenged both sides in the white community to stand aside as Blacks registered to vote or risk alienating potential Black voters. Within the city limits, Chief Harvey and the voter registrar did nothing to impede registration, but in most rural areas white resistance to Black people voting remained strong.

The four of us set out on an ambitious plan to reach every potential Black voter in the county. This was a plausible goal within the city limits of Kosciusko, where much of the work had already been done. It was not realistic to think we could visit every one of the hundreds of homes occupied by Black people in the rural areas of the county, where most houses were remote and could only be reached on a network of dirt roads.

We did have a huge map printed by the State Highway Department, Traffic and Planning Division, nailed to the wall of the Freedom House. It purported to show every primitive road and every house in the county. The map was two years old and was based on aerial photographs from 1962. We added information to it as we went along and Luther was able to pencil in some additional dirt roads, but much of the outlying region, particularly in the southeast portion of the county, remained unknown to us.

We did our best. We tried. We networked with people and let them tell us who might be open to a visit. The four of us from the Freedom House had at least one team of two people go out almost every day in July. We usually traveled in the car that was registered to Gunter, but we were often lent cars and even a pickup truck by neighbors. We sometimes had the Mallett family truck, which Luther was allowed to drive.

Luther and I usually were paired together. There were also times I went out paired with Gunter, but Luther and I got used to working as a team. As we visited homes Luther often had some family or friendship connection that would start a conversation. "I believe I went to school at Tipton with your cousin, Jimmy Esters. How's he doing?" People became comfortable with the two of us fairly easily. Doors opened to us when Luther provided a family connection.

It was on these daily trips that I came to understand how completely the Black community took care of us. Luther drove us through farmland on the outskirts of Kosciusko and on dirt roads that cut through the rural areas around Ethel and McCool. We drove from home to home without using the more traveled asphalt highways that crossed the county. On any road we were at risk, but we felt safer on dirt roads in predominantly Black areas where there was little traffic. As we passed low-cut crops on cultivated fields and crossed rivers and creeks, we watched for other cars, for anything out of the ordinary.

"Matt, you best be watching these dirt roads that come in from the side," would be Luther's reminder to me. I never let my attention stray during these drives. I marveled at the desolate beauty of the countryside, the light on the horizon flickering in the heat. The air smelled like sweet dirt. I watched for any movement, for any car that might be traveling within sight of us. We carried weapons in the open on the back seat, but we had no desire to use them. Reaching the next Black home usually meant reaching the next safe haven.

People were always cordial, even those who were still afraid. Luther and I walking up to a home together was often the moment when the civil rights movement had arrived at someone's front door. At first we stood on the porch and talked, one of us watching the road. Often we were invited inside and offered tea or lemonade.

Some people we met were skeptical that Black people would be allowed to register without being bothered by some white person. We could not guarantee anyone's safety, but we always said that the more people who registered, the safer it would be for everyone. We talked to people about the upcoming vote on alcohol, telling them this was a good time to register. We carried the forms and explained how to fill them out.

When people warmed to us, we were invited inside. Once we sat down in a house it became a visit, and any visit involved an offer of food. Women in the Black community fed the civil rights movement throughout the South. There were always snacks and tea. If it was lunch time, we were offered sandwiches or whatever was available. If Luther and I were out around six or seven at night, it was time for dinner. Maybe we were just lucky, or maybe Luther had a knack for finding the right house when it was time to eat. We'd be invited in for dinner and we were always well fed.

Canvassing did carry risk. One day I was paired with Gunter and we spent the day trying to talk to sharecroppers about registering to vote. Gunter took one of the asphalt roads and drove for about 30 minutes. At some point we turned off the highway and took a dirt road heading south. He slowed down, not as familiar with this area. We were two white men in a car with Mississippi plates, so the only threat to us would be if we were recognized. Gunter did present as unique, too tall to just fit in. He slouched as he drove.

Gunter's height could be a problem. Two unknown white men walking up to the home of a Black sharecropper was not a welcome sight, and Gunter at full height was intimidating. Many men would squat while talking together in rural Mississippi, and Gunter would be the first to squat if we were in a situation where his height might be a barrier. Squatting required him to look up to the person he was speaking to, an obvious gesture of deference. If we got into a good conversation, we might all be squatting.

One time an old white man in a white straw hat walked up on such a conversation, coming upon us from a path through the fields. His fields. The sharecropper lived on this man's land and farmed it. Gunter and I were trespassing. The sharecropper stood up quickly, lowered his head to the man with the straw hat and backed away more than a few steps.

"What do you think you're doin' here?" the white man said to us with a glare.

I was already standing, speechless. Gunter uncoiled slowly like a rattlesnake rising to its full height, his eyes holding the stare of the white man as he rose. The white man glared right back at him. Once Gunter was at his full height, he kept the gaze but spoke in quiet, calm tone.

"Sir, we're just here to talk about voting."

"Well you get yourself off my land, you hear? My boy ain't got no interest in talking to the likes of you. Go on, get."

"We understand."

I made very brief eye contact with the sharecropper, and Gunter and I backed away and reached the car. While we drove away I looked out of the back window with cautious eyes.

We mixed canvassing with networking among people in the rural areas of the county. Though most people were welcoming, and you could feel the network growing, not every home visit was a joyous event. There were folks who were ill, more than a few who were distracted by crying children, and once or twice someone who was drunk. Luther and I worked together most days, and after dark we sometimes went out with Gunter to destroy Klan signs in the county. I continued to stay at the Winfreys' house, sleeping on the couch and living like one of the family.

A few nights a week Luther and I stayed at the Freedom House on guard duty while Gunter and Betty went out to meet with people. The phone rang often and was a mixed blessing. My parents, white men threatening us, local activists, my friend Wendy, my parents again, Aaron Condon, my friend David Saft from New York, and again my parents. My mother would call every time she read anything about trouble anywhere in Mississippi, even if someone was arrested hundreds of miles away.

"Are you okay?" she would ask impatiently.

"I'm fine."

"Just fine? What's wrong?"

"Look, I'm fine, okay?" I responded with some irritation.

At one point I told her she was making more harassing phone calls to us than the Ku Klux Klan. She said I had no idea what it was like to be a parent with a child doing what I was doing.

A high point in our organizing was a visit on July 14 from Lawrence Guyot, chairman of the MFDP. It mattered that someone from Jackson was paying attention to the local community's efforts to organize. Born in Mississippi, at age 26 Guyot was a former SNCC organizer widely known for his courage. He stayed with the movement after being brutally beaten in 1963 in Winona, Mississippi while trying to bail Fannie Lou Hamer out of jail, at the same time as she was being beaten close to death in her cell. Now, three years later, his physical bulk conveyed a strength that was matched by his emotional calm.

Guyot came to town for a mass meeting at the Wesley Methodist Church, Rev. B.F. Harper presiding. Albert Truss offered to do guard duty at the Freedom House, allowing Gunter, Betty, Luther and me to all attend. The pews in the dark wooden interior of the church were filled with almost a hundred people, our largest movement gathering to date. The chapel buzzed with excitement.

"Did you know that in 1890 there were 189,000 registered Black voters in our state?" Guyot began. "There has not been a single colored person elected to office here since 1892, when Black voters were tossed off the registration books and only 8,600 remained. In just two years! We aim to reverse that trend. When the MFDP was formed in 1964 we estimate there were 28,500 Black voters in the state. At the beginning of this year that number was at least 117,000. Want that number to continue to grow? We want you, your neighbors, your friends, we want everyone to register to vote."

While most of rural Attala was Baptist, the Black community in Kosciusko was largely Methodist. Wesley Methodist was the largest Black church in the city. The meeting was perhaps more restrained than it might have been in a Baptist church, but that fit Guyot's speaking style just fine. It was never said that he lacked passion, but he could be more conversational than rousing, letting the facts themselves be provocative.

Guyot closed with an endorsement of Dock Drummond's campaign for a congressional seat from District One and called for a vote for Clifton

Whitely for senate against James O. Eastland, the notorious racist who had been in office since 1942. The crowd rose to give him a standing ovation and joined hands to sing "We Shall Overcome." We believed it.

On August 2 the vote on alcohol in Attala County was razor-thin. Of the 4,240 votes cast, 2,280 supported keeping the county dry, while 1,960 favored going wet, a difference of only 320 votes. Since the new local option law allowed the issue to be on the ballot again in two years, both sides in the white community now had an ongoing interest in courting the Black vote.

Chapter 16:
Small Town in the Central Hills

Attala was a county with one city, Kosciusko, and a few small towns. The rest of the county was farmland and forests, meadows and waterways, rivers, brooks and creeks. As we worked to extend the movement, we reached out to the small towns scattered throughout the central hills, like Ethel, McAdams and Sallis. One man brought us to McCool, with a population of 211. Nash Hannah came to a civil rights meeting in Kosciusko and invited the Freedom House people to his home.

When we first started going to McCool in late June, I was nervous. It had a reputation among Black people as the meanest place in the county. I heard tales of lynchings, rapes, assaults on Black women and strictly enforced rules of white supremacy that reached back to the end of Reconstruction.

We got to McCool by driving 18 miles northeast from Kosciusko on Highway 12, through flat, grassy farmland and hills full of pine trees. The road followed the Yockanookany River on our left as it flowed toward the Pearl River basin, but you couldn't see the river from the car window. Every mile or so we passed a farmhouse set back from the road. A few dogs kept a watchful eye from the shade of a porch. For long stretches it felt like we were driving through wilderness.

The first time the four of us, Gunter, Betty, Luther and I, made the trip, we went directly to Nash Hannah's home. To reach his house we turned north off Highway 12 on a dirt road we followed for almost a mile. It led us to a long dirt driveway leading up the side of a small hill. Two dogs started barking as we drove up to the house. Nash came out on the front porch, a rifle at his side. He saw who we were and greeted us.

"Quiet!" he ordered the German shepherds, who simmered down and came over to smell us. I had been bitten as a child and I wanted to keep my distance.

"Don't worry none about the dogs," he said, noticing my discomfort. "They can even get used to a white man. Glad you made it out here."

A muscular man in his late forties, Nash was self-confident in a way that was considered inappropriate at times by whites. He was polite, but not deferential. He was a veteran of World War II. Many Black men who returned to the Deep South after serving in the military could not accept returning to subservient status, and they often played important roles in the civil rights movement.

Nash made a living hauling lumber with his own truck, giving him some measure of independence and the ability to care financially for his family. We entered his home, welcomed by his wife and one child who was at home. We were offered something to drink. I remember sitting in the living room, relaxing in a very comfortable chair, as Betty and Gunter chatted with the family and Luther and I took in the surroundings, a spacious and solid living room with a large couch and at least three easy chairs. I was thankful to be out of the heat, drinking lemonade, the cold glass itself a wonderful sensation in my hands.

"Hard to believe," Nash said, "but many years ago this was a boom town. The railroad ran through here, and there was plenty of cotton and timber. At one time there were even four saloons." He laughed. "No more. No more prosperity either. A few white families own most of the land. Most Black people here do farm labor. The two stores downtown only serve Blacks who come to the door for colored people. It can get plenty rough in this area. In some ways it's as bad as Neshoba County."

It took a lot of conversation to figure out how to connect people in the area who might be ready to register to vote and those ready to join the movement. Nash was a natural organizer because he understood people: who was ready to step forward and who was still controlled by fear, how particular people might feel if we came to their door. We talked about community connections, who belonged to which church, how people were related as family, who worked together, anything that linked the community together.

That day, our little group, Black and white, sitting together in the heat of a Mississippi summer afternoon, came to agree that the civil rights movement could take root in McCool. If we could be a presence here, if we could openly challenge the grip of white power and build a movement here, the entire county would know.

The four of us who had driven from Kosciusko also knew, or perhaps it was Betty and Gunter who came up with the plan, that what we had to do to announce our presence here was to enter the downtown stores as an integrated group.

The next time the four of us came to town we again drove on Highway 12 until we reached the turnoff marked McCool. Downtown emerged as we came around a bend in the road. What was left of downtown McCool consisted of a post office opened in 1883, a wooden sidewalk, and two brick stores built in 1905. Each store had two entrances, one for whites and the other for everybody else. They were owned by the Bowie brothers, Robert Neal Bowie, who with his wife, Katherine, ran a general store called Bowie's Grocery and Café, and E.B. Bowie, who ran Bowie's City Café and Grocery.

We parked on the side of the dirt road, the town seemingly deserted in the heat. The two stores sat side by side. The four of us crossed the street to the porch of the City Café and Grocery, which had two doors at the front entrance. We entered together. Betty strode in, followed by Gunter. Luther and I were close behind them, watching the street, but there were no people, no cars, no motion at all except our swirl of energy. I was glad I had double-tied the laces on my shoes, in case we had to run.

When we entered, E.B. Bowie was standing behind the café counter. A muscled but aging man, he had been born in McCool in 1901, a descendant of early white settlers in the area after it was taken from the Choctaws. It was said that this Bowie let it be known that any civil rights worker who dared to enter his store would feel the weight of his axe handle. Betty may have been the first Black person to ever walk through the door reserved exclusively for white people. E.B. glared at us and clenched his hands.

"Get the hell outta here. I ain't serving no niggers in my place."

It was Gunter who responded, in a quiet but assertive tone.

"I'm sure you don't want any trouble. We just want to order."

"The hell you do." E.B. replied, but his tone was changing, from an aggressive challenge to what seemed more like a statement of fact.

By this time Betty had taken a seat at the counter. E.B. seemed ready to burst, but he didn't reach for an axe handle. It helped that there were four of us, and it may have helped that Gunter was now well known in the county, with a reputation for being unpredictable. The rest of us sat down.

E.B. was so angry he didn't seem to notice or care how scared I was at that moment, as I kept an eye on the front door and an eye on E.B. "Colas for all of us," Betty said firmly.

E.B. put the bottles on the counter along with a bottle opener, and let us take them ourselves. He never took his eyes off us, and he certainly was not going to serve us, but to his credit he charged us the posted price. We paid, drank the sodas in a silent combination of tension and celebration, and walked out.

We had probably spent only ten minutes inside the store, and we hadn't changed Bowie's system, but we had made a statement and made our presence known.

During this period, most nights I continued to spend some time at the Freedom House and slept at the Winfreys' house. Luther lived at home. He and I continued driving to the area around McCool on a regular basis. We traveled on back roads leading to rural households and farms. We started out visiting specific people who knew Nash Hannah. He led us to folks inclined to step forward, so long as they weren't stepping forward alone. We used the same method of networking Betty and Gunter had used successfully when they first arrived.

We brought sample voter registration forms with us everywhere. Every house we visited was different, every family situation unique. We were visiting some older couples, a few single people, and many families with young children crowded into small shacks. There were always times when people were just being deferential to us, or polite, or looking for an easy way to exit the conversation.

Most visits felt positive, with people pleased to be treated with respect and curious about meeting two of the civil rights workers they'd been hearing about. Some visits were stirring, when it felt as if the household had been waiting to be touched by the civil rights movement. There were times we had long chats outside, squatting in the dust.

In the privacy of their homes people spoke more freely about what it meant to challenge the rules in Mississippi. What were the real risks of trying to register to vote? What had happened to other people who had tried? We could always mention Nash Hannah and soon Robert Lowry and Everlee Pullam and the Dotson family as people who had success-fully registered. There was the risk of retaliation by the white community, but with the pending whisky vote whites so far were accepting Black registration.

We traveled to McCool a few days a week. There were days when Luther went out with Gunter, and Betty might be in a small meeting at someone's home, or days when Luther might be needed at home and I would travel with Gunter. It seemed to me we functioned well as a small group, at that time and in that setting, helping to calm the pervasive fear for our own safety each of us felt every day.

Some afternoons I stayed at the Freedom House, taking phone calls and visiting with people who came over to chat. Usually a few high school students hung out on the front porch or in the shade of the front room. We never had any kind of freedom school, or any thought about creating one, but there was a time we received a book of lyrics of freedom songs from up North. I tried to lead a session of singing, but thankfully Wiley took over after one or two songs, and after that things were lively.

One morning our visitor was James Meredith, born in Kosciusko and in town to visit his mother Roxie. He wore his trademark yellow pith helmet and was in the company of a young Black man carrying a microphone, cameras and audio equipment. At first, Gunter did much of the talking. Meredith was friendly and interested in what was happening in town. I learned that he too was a veteran, having served in the Air Force before returning to his home state and applying to the University of Mississippi.

Meredith had a reputation for being independent and strong-willed. He didn't seem to care what anyone thought about the pith helmet. He was not part of the MFDP or CORE or any other civil rights organization. "This is about war," he said to us as we stood outside and talked. "This is not about civil rights. This is about white supremacy and the fear that keeps white supremacy in power." He didn't come inside and I never saw him again, but I was pleased that he shook our hands when he left.

One evening we had a visitor who did come inside, a young white teenager who had been calling on the phone for weeks. Many calls from whites were hostile, but this young man had been friendly and curious. He showed up alone. It was startling to have a white Mississippian inside our house, but there was nothing threatening in his body language or his tone of voice.

For almost an hour he sat on one of the cots, his head leaning against the wall, as we talked cautiously about race. We touched on an attempted justification for white supremacy based on the biblical Curse of Ham, We talked candidly about the daily abuse of Black people. We heard from him that other young whites talked about coming to the Freedom House, but were either afraid of us or afraid of what other whites would think of them. That was the only time we saw him.

Mr. and Mrs. Winfrey continued to open their home to me at night, taking care of me and asking nothing in return. One morning there were visitors, two Black women in their twenties. I know now that it was Kate, one of Mr. and Mrs. Winfrey's daughters, and one of her classmates from college in Itta Bena. They were both very interested in what was happening with civil rights in Kosciusko. We shared breakfast and talked about the county and about the movement. Everyone in the family had a concern. Mr. Winfrey was particularly concerned about our trips to McCool. "You be careful out there," was his frequent admonition.

We were careful, but we were persistent. Luther and I worked closely with Nash Hannah, and as we continued canvassing we spent two or three nights at his home. He had dug a trench at an angle to the driveway, using the dirt to form a barrier against bullets and explosives, and we took turns in the trench while guarding his house. In the morning we were roused by strong coffee and a plentiful breakfast.

One long dirt road took us through a pine forest to the farmhouse of Tathilia Gaston, a Black woman in her sixties who was friends with Nash Hannah and one of the first Black people in McCool to register to vote. She had some French ancestry and a chiseled, angular face. Wearing an ankle-length dress and a bandanna, she was slightly stooped over when she walked. She loved to chat with us, often quoting Bible stories to us while serving us something cold to drink. We were able to help her with a problem with Social Security by sending information to movement lawyers in Jackson, and she took us in as if we were her kin. Her husband, Giles Gaston, stayed in the background, but he too registered to vote.

We started visiting people who were members of Mrs. Gaston's Baptist church. The idea, after reaching out to friends of Nash Hannah, was to build a network of people by connecting folks who were already linked by church communities, family relationships and social attitudes.

Within a few weeks we got permission to hold McCool's first civil rights meeting at a partially abandoned church called the White Plains Baptist Church, an old wooden-frame church set on a hillside in the forest. It had been a church for the local Black Baptist community for decades, though the man who gave us the keys said he hadn't been inside for a year. Luther and I spent an afternoon sweeping it clean. We all knew there was a risk that having a civil rights meeting there could lead to the church being burned to the ground. The congregation was willing to take that risk.

We put out a leaflet announcing the meeting and passed it out when we canvassed home to home. Thirty-two people came.

Betty, Dock Drummond and Nash Hannah ran the meeting. The conversation was about registering to vote and taking steps to change McCool. Gunter, Luther and I played no role inside the church. Our role was protecting the meeting. The dirt road which passed in front of the church was the only road in and the only road out. The three of us spread out across the hillside as the meeting began, each of us armed. I was again carrying the .22 rifle. We waited for the arrival of the Klan.

The first cars appeared within minutes.

Two late model Fords packed with white men with guns drove very slowly in front of the church, like armadillos sprouting gun barrels. Rifles and shotguns protruded from the car windows as one driver pointed his upraised middle finger at us. They were joined by a third car and continued to drive by the church as the meeting continued.

I never saw the men in the cars point their weapons at us, and we kept our guns pointed to the ground. They circled slowly, drove away, disappeared for short stretches of time, then reappeared, driving by on the dirt road, staring at us. We shifted among the trees as we watched them. If their goal was to jangle our nerves, it worked on me. Every time they drove past, I sought the thin protection of a pine tree and prepared for shots to be fired.

As the meeting ended, I felt the tension rise when people started to emerge from the church. Though not a shot had been fired, everyone quickly knew about the cars full of white men who had been driving back and forth during the meeting. Folks were quiet and watchful as they left the church, eyes glancing at the road, small gestures motioning folks to their vehicles.

Where were the white men? Were they waiting somewhere?

Small caravans left the driveway as people headed home. Nash Hannah made sure each group included someone who was armed. After we closed up the church, Luther got in a car with Betty and Dock Drummond. I became the front seat passenger in the car driven by Gunter. There would be no integrated vehicles leaving this hillside meeting.

Driving with Gunter was an act of pure faith. He was impulsive, sometimes speeding on instinct, and as his passenger I had to trust that he would make the right decision at a moment's notice. He would need to know if I saw any danger, but he was the one who would have to react. We put our rifles on the dashboard, two pistols on the back seat, in clear sight and within reach, and headed down the dirt road through the woods back to Highway 12.

There were no white men lurking in cars, no one waiting for us. No one fired at us. The dirt road took us through the pine forest in peace. We reached the asphalt and turned left, heading away from the meeting and traveling though the hills toward Kosciusko. I stared out the back window. I saw nothing. Gunter kept to the speed limit and watched the road ahead of us. I let myself breathe. We had made it out safely.

Suddenly a car appeared behind us, briefly visible at the crest of the last rise in the road. "Car behind us," I said. Gunter added the pistol from his waistband to the collection on the backseat and hit the gas. I reached for my rifle and watched the car behind us fade from view. The next rise brought another glimpse. They were gaining on us, and I got ready for what seemed surely to be a gunfight as we raced for town.

The car reappeared, accelerating as it rushed directly at us. I got a better look. There were lights flashing on the roof. "Gunter, it's the police."

"What?" he said with annoyance. "Why are they coming after us?"

We pulled over on the side of the road. The local constable pulled in behind us, got out of his car and came over to Gunter.

"You best keep your hands off those guns. You fellas coming from that meeting over at White Plains Church?"

We were under arrest. The charge was "pointing and aiming a deadly weapon." Apparently some of the white men who had circled the meeting claimed we had aimed our rifles at them. The constable placed us in the back of his car and drove us to the county jail, one block from the

Kosciusko town square. It was the only jail in the county and was also used by the city police. We were photographed and booked.

I was irritated that I was being hauled in on a lie. I was learning the truth of something James Meredith had said, that in Mississippi one can just as easily be arrested for not committing a crime as for committing a crime. In my irritation, I tried to make things difficult for the man who was taking my fingerprints. Every time he tried to roll one of my fingers in the ink, I bent that finger at the joint. Every time he tried to roll an inked finger on police paper, I spread out all my fingers so my hand couldn't roll. After working out my irritation on him, I realized there was no point to what I was doing, and when I cooperated he finally got all ten fingers inked and printed.

The city police seemed surprised that I had been arrested by the constable and left me sitting on a bench. At one point I was placed alone in the drunk tank, a cement cell with no windows, but a different police officer quickly took me out and brought me back to the bench. I soon learned that I wasn't being charged with anything. The white men in McCool had been only able to identify "fuzzy" in their allegation, but they had no idea who I was and none of them could identify Luther. I waited while Betty arranged to have Gunter bailed out.

Betty and Gunter decided the three of us should stay together, in case there were more repercussions from the meeting in McCool. I spent that night at the Freedom House.

The dirt road used by white attackers
to enter and flee the Black community.
Photo by the author

Fire at the Freedom House

Chapter 17:
Night Falls

When night fell it always brought an edge of danger. The world changed for civil rights workers and the Black community when the sun went down. Darkness allowed people to sneak around unseen. The cover of night brought out foolishness and revenge and all manner of surprise. Darkness brought out night riders.

I was occasionally alone at the Freedom House when night fell, on guard duty in the front room. The phone might ring. The calls after dark were rarely friendly.

"You that nigger-loving white trash?"

"Who am I speaking with?"

"Don't give me none of that. We're comin' to get you."

Click.

The phone would ring again.

"You that nigger-loving race traitor?"

"Didn't I just talk with you?"

"I don't know who you been talkin' with. You that fella from New York? You sure sound like it."

"Yeah, I'm from New York. You want to talk about it?"

"Don't need to."

Click.

We had been getting calls like this ever since the new phone book for Attala County was issued on July 5, listing the Freedom House after Fred's Dollar Store and before Freeman's Truck Line. Our phone number had gone public.

I was alone at the Freedom House when Luther was home with his family and Betty and Gunter were off somewhere. At first it was fine with me to be alone. I didn't mind the solitude or the quiet, but these calls drove me outside, worried and alert.

After most of these phone calls I would step out, not lingering on the porch but heading down the steps to the dry dirt. Often I would pace the ground on the side of the house or walk to the hillside, where I would hide among the trees when any cars drove past. I could usually see who was inside a car with light from nearby houses and on some nights with light from the moon. I tried to remain cautious, but it could be difficult to stay focused after three or four hours of guard duty.

I always carried a weapon when I was in this situation, usually the .22 caliber rifle, although a shotgun was available. It was a pump shotgun which could be loaded with multiple shells and fired multiple times by sliding the pump on the barrel. The .22 rifle was the same one I had used during the winter. It fired just a single shot at a time, but it was my weapon of choice if I wanted any chance of accuracy. Both guns cried out to be fired.

I found it very tempting to shoot the rifle while holding it night after night, in the dark, when it seemed nothing was happening but something could happen at any moment. When I carried the .22, it seemed so familiar, so ready to fire, I would put my finger on the trigger and slowly start to squeeze it. I had no target. I wasn't aiming the gun at anything, I was just playing with the trigger, squeezing it, releasing it, slowly squeezing harder, feeling for that edge where squeezing would release the firing pin.

Bam! The explosion of gunpowder slammed into my ears. The rifle seemed to fire by itself. I was holding the gun loosely when I squeezed the trigger and fired that shot, the barrel pointed at the ground. At that moment I could have become known as the civil rights worker who shot himself in the foot. Fortunately the bullet hit the dirt and missed my feet completely.

Silence followed the shot. After a minute or two Mrs. Nash opened her front door.

"It's okay," I called to her, as I looked around and crossed the road to her, still holding the rifle. I explained what had happened.

She looked at me sternly. "Son, that sure won't happen again."

"No, ma'am."

Gunter and Betty returned later that night and Gunter drove me back to the Winfreys' house on North Natchez Street. I never mentioned the incident.

Guns for self-defense were everywhere in the Black community. At one point I bought a .38 Smith & Wesson revolver to carry with me at night. The sale was for cash in someone's living room, an elderly Black man with an extra gun he was willing to sell to the movement, unregistered and off the books, a sure sign we were beginning to stretch the limits. I had it with me the few times I walked back to the Winfrey home on my own.

Carrying a gun gave me an illusion of safety. I took at least one risk carrying that revolver that I would never have otherwise considered, one night when passing by the Highway 12 Standard gas station. I was on the series of paths and dirt roads I used to reach the Winfreys' North Natchez Street house.

I started thinking about the metal "Colored" sign the station had screwed on the door to the back bathroom.

In those days we were trained to carry ten cents at all times, two nickels or a dime. Your car might break down, or you might get delayed while canvassing or you might always get arrested. In those days unless you had access to a house phone, the only way to make a call was from a pay phone, usually at a gas station or a business, and a pay phone cost ten cents. I always had a dime in the front pocket of my dungarees.

The wonderful thing about the dime is its size. It easily doubles as a screwdriver, just the tool I needed to take down the "Colored" sign in the back of the Standard station, closed for the night. I knew at the time that I was skirting the edge of being reckless, and I was probably wrong about which side of that line I was on. I watched the road, prepared my alibi ("I'm just back here trying to use the bathroom") and walked past the side of the service station and the "White Ladies" restroom, into the darkness and quiet at the back of the station. The dime fit perfectly in the grooves of the metal screws, and in a minute the sign was off the door and hidden in my dungarees.

I took the sign with me as I walked back to the Winfrey home, still watching to see if anyone was watching me. I never mentioned my acquisition to the Winfreys. There was no reason to make them complicit in any way, and I got the sign out of their house in the morning. At the first opportunity I mailed it North to my friend David, who lived in that most hated of Northern urban centers, New York City.

The sign never appeared on the back bathroom door again. The two front bathrooms were integrated by October, the old "Colored" bathroom was closed and the room was used for storage.

Darkness one night brought an unanticipated danger. Luther and I returned to the Freedom House after a day of canvassing to find Gunter and Betty waiting for us anxiously. It was difficult at first to comprehend what we were being told, since it involved bombs and stolen guns and an integrated group of people camping on land in the county.

"These people are here in Attala County and they're talking about setting off bombs. They've been around the state and the movement. They think they can spark an armed revolution." Gunter started out. "For some reason, they're here."

"Gunter," Betty spoke up, "you know word is one of them is John Handy, who's already been thrown out by the Delta Ministry. I don't give a damn why they're here. They gotta go and they gotta give up this stupidity."

They stared at each other. It was a wordless communication in a relationship I never fully understood, even when they spoke to each other in my presence. Sometimes they had fights over what seemed like nothing, sometimes they were openly warm and affectionate. I had never before lived around a couple, except my parents and grandparents, and I had no sense of what caused tension between Gunter and Betty. That night whatever was at issue between them got resolved and Gunter turned his attention to me and Luther.

"Look, we've gotten word these people are serious about these bombs. We need to go out there and have a talk with them."

Within a few minutes Luther and I were in the car with Gunter, heading out to some remote area to confront people who were living in a tent. Betty stayed behind to guard the Freedom House.

Gunter took us on a series of dirt roads, unfamiliar to me. Luther seemed to know where we were when we turned left near a small cemetery. He looked at me and nodded silently while we kept watch for our daily enemies, the white racists and Klansmen who might be out at night. A large tent appeared in the distance in front of us, its walls shinning from the bright lights inside. We could see the silhouettes of a pickup truck and one or two cars parked in front.

"Do we have a plan here?" Luther asked.

"Don't worry," Gunter replied. "I'll talk to them."

"No, that's not it," Luther said. "Look, pull up in front of that truck, near the entrance. I'll be the first one they see and, if we need to, we can get out of here fast."

I understood what Luther was thinking. Movement people in the Deep South would be surprised but not frightened by the sudden appearance of an unknown Black man, while the sudden appearance of an unknown white man would trigger alarm.

We parked and Luther led the way into a large canvas tent, big enough for a small circus and set out like a command post. The lanterns were so bright it felt like we were inside a house. There were green military cots, a large folding table and boxes and crates of supplies. A few rifles were stacked in a corner, but what really caught my eye were open wooden crates filled with what looked like either flares or actual dynamite.

Four adults, three men and one woman, were startled by our entrance, but they reacted quickly. In less than a minute everyone in the tent had a weapon. Luther held a shotgun and I had the .22 rifle, which I was holding very carefully. Gunter kept his hand on the pistol in his waistband.

Two groups of apparent strangers, seven armed people, were all watching each other, alert to movement of any kind. The racial make-up of this confrontation defied all norms, as both groups were a mixture of Black and white. The only woman in the tent was white, and she was the first to speak.

"Well, hello Gunter. What the hell are you up to?"

Gunter just glared at her. A young Black man standing behind the folding table took charge. "Hey Gunter, you and your friends are not welcome here. Your time has passed. Now it's the time of tooth for tooth."

"No, that's not the way it's going down," said Gunter, trying to dominate the space with his height and tone of voice. "Nobody wants you here. That goes for you too, Emily."

Luther and I watched as the scene played out. Clearly there was some personal history here. The fact that these three knew each other helped all of us relax. Two groups of armed movement people, facing off in a tent, was transformed into a verbal disagreement among these three.

In the argument that followed, the two tent people spoke forcefully for armed revolution, arguing that the time had come for setting off bombs "to rattle the teeth of the racists." Gunter replied with equal fierceness that the civil rights movement in the county was ready for self-defense, including self-defense against anybody setting off bombs.

The verbal confrontation continued, but the tone slowly became calmer and I stopped listening to the words. My attention was focused on watching the other people in the tent. As the fear of imminent violence began to fade, shoulders softened and hands became more relaxed on weapons. The argument ended with Gunter being told he was worthless and Gunter warning the group to get out of the county. We were able to walk to the car unmolested and drive away.

Once in the car we couldn't stop talking. "What the hell was that?" asked Luther. "Those were some scary people. They look to me like they're already on the run." I agreed. "Was that real? Were those actual bombs?" I asked, trying to figure out if those were really explosives we had seen or just flares that looked like sticks of dynamite. None of us were sure.

When we got back to Betty, she got the whole story in fits and starts from the three of us. She didn't seem surprised by any of it. "I've seen this nonsense before," she said. "It gets everybody riled up and it goes nowhere."

We learned the next day that the tent and the people in it were gone. I never heard about them again, not in Mississippi or anywhere else, but I thought about them for many nights. The experience rattled me. While I felt emotionally prepared for armed conflict with white racists, it was apocalyptic to think about violent conflict within the movement itself.

It was Betty who saw that the strain was building in me. I was edgy. There were times I would jump when the phone rang or when there was a sudden noise. Early one evening she took me by surprise.

"Hey, Matt," she said. "I got a friend who wants to go to Durant with us. Let's go listen to some music."

Durant was about 20 miles to the northwest on Highway 12, in Holmes County, just across the county border on the other side of the Big Black River. It was a stop on the Illinois Central Railroad and had a stately brick depot. At times it was a major social center and a first step for many joining the migration to the North. It also had more than a few juke joints.

A juke joint in the Black community was a place that played music, often live, and invited people to kick back, socialize, have a few drinks and dance. "Juke" was said to be the word for music derived from the African Gullah language. Many places played free music from a "jukebox," the name given to "partially automated music-playing devices" when they became widespread in the South. We knew you could get moonshine in the juke joints in Durant. It was a common destination at night for people from Kosciusko. How could I pass up this opportunity?

Once again Albert Truss guarded the Freedom House. The four of us drove west on Highway 12, two guns on the seats. The road was quiet and lovely; stars were shining in a clear sky on a calm night. We crossed the river on a short bridge and entered Holmes County. One left turn past the train depot took us to the G&G Trick Me Lounge, a small brick and mortar building painted lime green on the outside.

The inside of the Trick Me, in contrast, was dim and easy on the eyes. There was a long wooden bar, six or seven round tables with wooden chairs and a dance floor worn smooth by decades of swirling, gliding, pounding feet. Photographs and posters announcing concerts and events decorated the walls. Red light bulbs glowed from behind the bar.

Music from the jukebox filled the air. This was not guitar picking from the Delta. This was not the traditional blues played on the radio the first time I came to the state, driving south from Memphis. The jukebox was not playing gospel music or the freedom songs that brought life and energy to the movement. It played dancing music. This was Motown.

Our entrance hardly caused a ripple. Here we were, two white men with two Black women, often an expression of white power and oppression, yet we didn't catch stares or hostile glances. It could have been that Betty and Gunter were regulars. It may have been that folks in Durant were used to seeing civil rights workers by this time, since Holmes County had a long history of activism. It certainly mattered that the women carried themselves with their heads held high and a bearing that seemed to say, "We're here with these white guys because we want to be, and that's all there is to say about it."

It was a night of music and dancing. The Trick Me filled within an hour, the tables packed and people at the bar and lining the walls. After a few drinks and music from the juke box like the latest from Percy Sledge or Jimmy Ruffin's newly released "What Becomes of the Brokenhearted," we were treated to a live band. They played a mix of blues and rock 'n' roll that Betty called boogie music. The crowd was there to party and party we did.

This was not like any party I had ever been to in Valley Stream or Oberlin or even Morgan State College. People were fluid, graceful and smooth, sensual and exuberant. At first I felt awkward with Betty's friend, but that changed. Once out on the floor, I felt welcomed and embraced.

The four of us returned to Kosciusko without incident. Gunter drove. There was no problem with other cars on the road or with his driving, though he had consumed his share of moonshine. We crossed the Big Black River and returned to Attala County. The farms we drove past were settled and calm. The road to the Freedom House felt familiar and safe. I felt secure. The night at the juke joint had taken the edge off my anxiety.

Albert Truss was outside, always vigilant, ready to greet us. It had been a peaceful evening. A message had come in for me on the phone. Alan Moonves, whom we had last seen during the Memorial marches in Neshoba County, had called from Louisiana. I needed to call him in the morning.

Alan Moonves in Washington, D.C.
Photo by the author

Fire at the Freedom House

Chapter 18:
Jason Niles Park

It was early in the morning, but the phone was ringing. It was Alan. "Matt, I really need to get out of here." He was calling from a CORE organizing project in Ferriday, Louisiana, an impoverished town on the other side of the Mississippi River, across from Natchez. "The project here is falling apart. The Klan runs the town. I need to get out of here. Can you use more civil rights workers where you are?"

Alan Moonves was one of my best friends growing up in Valley Stream. He had joined Long Island CORE with me in 1963. We had both been assigned by CORE to be street marshals during the huge Harlem demonstrations in support of the struggle in Selma, Alabama. We had been encouraged to develop an inner toughness.

Now we were both in the Deep South. Alan had gone to Louisiana in early June to work with CORE, but they had immediately sent him to join the Meredith March. Luther and I had spoken with him briefly in Neshoba County, where I had given him the Freedom House phone number. Alan had been gassed and beaten by the police in Canton, along with Wiley and Jean Mallett, although they did not know each other at the time. When the Meredith March ended, Alan had gone back to Louisiana and CORE had assigned him to Ferriday, which had a reputation for violence.

"I'm doing alright, but this is not working out. We can't keep a Freedom House open. Half the time I'm here alone. When there are other organizers in town we don't get along. There's a very brave family putting me up, but I need to move." Alan was emphatic. He said he also had a friend from college, Timothy, who was ready to come South. Could they both come to Attala County?

It was good to hear Alan's voice. After we had spoken for a few minutes, I told him I couldn't make the decision alone. I also told him we practiced armed self-defense, that in Mississippi Black people had been guarding their homes for years and staff people were now doing the same. Alan said armed self-defense was now CORE's official policy throughout Louisiana, and he was comfortable with it.

This was not an easy decision for the four of us. We knew there was some risk. Two new people of any color would be an adjustment. Two white guys, one new to the South, was a stretch. But Luther and I were eager to put more time into organizing around McCool, and to do that we needed more organizers. Betty was ready to take a chance on anyone who had worked with CORE. Gunter was more hesitant. He made some phone calls, spoke with local activists, then called Alan back and talked for about ten minutes. In the end, we all agreed to accept both Alan and Timothy. Gunter made plans to pick them up in Jackson.

The timing was perfect. They arrived the day before the vote on alcohol, one day of rest for them. Betty and Luther liked them and Alan bonded with Gunter immediately. The next day Alan and Timothy, paired with someone from the community, were able to work with local activists to get out the vote, going door to door simply reminding people that this was the day to vote.

Even though it had been a group decision, I felt responsible for Alan and Timothy being in Attala County. I was relieved that they seemed comfortable and were accepted by the Black community. They were deferential to people, particularly elders, and friendly with folks they were meeting for the first time. Timothy seemed awed by everything around him, not a surprising reaction to being in the Deep South for the first time, but he carried none of the arrogance sometimes seen in Northern white college students.

The vote on alcohol that day was very close. The county remained dry by a margin of just 320 votes. Though fear continued to cause many people in the rural sections of the county to hesitate, the hope in the city of Kosciusko was that the right to vote without fear of retribution was now within reach. The activists who had been singularly focused on the whisky vote as an opportunity for a voter registration drive were now ready to let other issues become the focus of the movement.

The spark that next ignited the community was the fight over access to the city swimming pool. There had been anticipation all summer among the high school students about trying to integrate the only swimming pool in Kosciusko, set outdoors in Jason Niles Park. There was no "separate but equal" swimming pool; there simply was no place at all for Black people to swim, not even a decent swimming hole in the muddy rivers that ran through the county. The same young people who had participated in integrating the cafés and the Strand were eager to take on the "whites only" swimming pool. They wanted to swim, or at least immerse themselves in the cold water of a pool.

These high school students had grown up watching the civil rights movement on TV, listening about it on the radio and seeing pictures of marches and demonstrations. They knew about the fight for school integration in Little Rock, the bus boycott in Montgomery, the Freedom Rides and the lunch counter sit-ins. They had seen their elders register to vote and many had been on the Meredith March or at least one of the marches in Neshoba County. They saw no reason to be patient.

On their own, students built a group at Tipton High School. When school let out and the summer heat arrived, people started talking about the swimming pool. If they could succeed with direct action to open up the movie theater, why not open up the pool? On their own initiative, a few had already picketed the park. While the students were pressing the issue of being barred from the pool, many adults in the MFDP worried about stirring up white anger during the voter registration drive. This tension was resolved with an understanding that the students would not take any direct action until after the vote on alcohol.

The students were willing to wait only one day. The whiskey vote took place on Tuesday. The demonstration at Jason Niles Park that had been talked about for weeks took place on Wednesday. The plan was to gather as many students as possible near the East Street entrance to the park, then enter as a group. If there was an arrest, no one wanted to go limp and be carried out of the park. Why give a white policeman the chance to hurt somebody? The plan was to accept arrest without resistance.

When we talked during a planning meeting, we realized we didn't know if we would even reach the pool, since there was a risk we would be arrested as soon as we crossed the East Street entrance. I thought the police would order us to leave and when we refused, look for some way to defuse the situation. We could not know if this action would succeed, but the adults in the movement agreed it was time. Some adults were being pushed by their children, who were impatient to try.

It was decided that Betty would remain at the Freedom House, near the phone and ready to take charge if we were all arrested. Gunter, Luther and I would be with the group that entered the park. After some discussion with Alan and Timothy, both said they were ready to join us. Betty would be in touch with a network of worried parents and with the Jackson office of the Lawyers Committee for Civil Rights Under Law. She also had contacts for bail money. We knew we were striking at a very emotional issue.

The pool had been open since the summer of 1955 and had become a special place for white families in the city. Many white children learned how to swim in the pool at Jason Niles Park with the help of the director of parks, A.D. McBeath. For them, this was a fond childhood memory. The park also had a teen center and was a fine place to relax and cool off on a hot summer day, but only if you were white.

Immersion in water can be experienced as a form of intimacy and bonding, as in communal baths and at public beaches. But in white culture in the United States in general, and particularly in the Deep South at that time, there was a visceral horror at the idea of being in a swimming pool with Black people. White people, North and South, talked about Black people as being dirty. It was a common experience for a white person to touch the skin of a Black person for the first time and glance at their hand to see if they picked up a stain. The idea of integrated swimming brought a sense of danger, a fear that people of color would leak some mysterious pigment into the pool, which would spread like ink in the water and cover the white folks, who would then emerge with black skin. These feelings ran very deep.

We gathered outside the park on August 3, another hot muggy day in Kosciusko, much like the day before and the day before that. *The Star-Herald* said it was 91 degrees, on its way to 94. The paper didn't bother to list humidity, which I think was because everybody just assumed it would be humid. It was a fine day to go swimming.

Many people walked over in groups of three or four, and when people stopped arriving after 11 a.m. there were 23 of us. Most of the young people were students from Tipton High. Luther seemed to know everybody. Wiley and Jean were there, as were Emma Ree Rayford, Shirley Yowk, Doris Yowk and Sarah Robinson. The Malletts were there with the blessing of their mother, and we hoped everyone had the support of family members.

Jason Niles was not a large park, perhaps the size of four large housing lots set aside on the edge of the white residential community just north of the town square. It was big enough for the outdoor pool and a teen center called the Dixieland Pavilion. Though one side of the park was on a slope, it was flat enough for a curved path with benches and folding umbrellas.

The park was completely empty when we walked in. This was odd and unexpected. It made the park feel ominous, as though some danger was lurking, waiting to pounce. There were no trees to shield us from the sun and the umbrellas were gone. It would have been wonderful to dip in some cool water, but when we actually reached the pool it was covered with a tarp. It was closed.

The white city government was so concerned about being forced to integrate the swimming pool that it was discussing closing it forever. It was thought by those who led the white community that the pool had to be sacrificed in order to protect the Southern Way of Life. The idea of sharing the pool with the Black community was never considered an option.

We found ourselves integrating an empty park. Perhaps the police department had hoped that we would simply leave, but so much effort had gone into gathering together that we took pleasure in simply being in a space that had been off-limits until that day. The only shade was around the teen center, so we gathered on the side of the building and talked in small groups.

This was the first chance Alan had to spend time with Wiley and Jean. They talked about being attacked by the police in Canton during the Meredith March, the panic during the attack and the stinging feeling of the tear gas. "It burned my face," Alan was saying. "I couldn't take a breath to even scream, and my eyes were on fire. I followed people around me to get away from the gas canisters."

"Yeah, at first I couldn't get away," Jean added. "One of those troopers even smiled when he pointed his bayonet at my neck." Wiley filled in the details of the troopers pushing people and tearing down the tents.

I could have gone on listening, but from the corner of my eye I saw one of the older students pulling on some screen or mosquito netting.

It was covering a sliding glass window which was partially open. I was probably 15 feet away as I watched him bend back the screen. I did not say a word. As I watched, he bent back the screen as far as possible, slid open the glass window and climbed inside. Within a minute he opened the front door and called out for people to join him.

Most everybody was hesitant. We had come to integrate the pool, not to break into the teen center. But wasn't integrating the center just as valid? After standing around wondering what to do once we saw that the pool was closed, the idea of going into the city teen center, never open to Black teens, seemed like another way to integrate the park. It was scary and thrilling at the same time. At first only a few people went in.

"Hey, Luther," I asked, "What do we do here?"

"Matt," he said without hesitation, "there's no way people should be in there without us."

By this time almost everyone was going inside, so we simply joined them. The teen center was musty, but at that moment it seemed wondrous. It wasn't large, but it was larger than any recreation center available to Black teens, since there were none. And there was shade from the heat. Most of us, myself included, just sat on the floor and leaned against the walls.

There was a table near the center of the room. It might have been a ping pong table, and somewhere there might be paddles and balls. Someone looked but found nothing. There was a small rubber ball that people tossed around. Mostly we just cooled off and got comfortable.

It started to be fun. We had all been tense when we first entered. Being outside in the eerie atmosphere of an empty park in the scorching sun had been uncomfortable, but now we could relax and even joke around.

Our revelry was short-lived. "The police are here," someone called from outside.

Chapter 19:
Afraid of Their Jail?

"Here they come."

Most of us were still inside the teen center, but we piled out of the door quickly as word spread. We could see two policemen sitting in a city police car on one side of the park. No one got out of the car.

"Who is it?" I asked Luther.

"Looks like Russell and Barton," he replied. "Probably trouble."

For a few moments it seemed possible nothing would happen. Maybe they were just taking a look, and would drive away. We held that hope in vain. One of them was already talking on his police radio.

In what felt like less than two minutes, more law enforcement arrived, at least four men from the Kosciusko Police Department with someone from the county sheriff's department. They came with two police cars, then a private truck and finally a school bus from the Attala County School District. This did not look good.

The presence of the school bus was the most ominous. It meant the police were thinking about taking us all. We were afraid, each in our own private way, but so far there was no physical threat. Some police glared at us, but they made no move toward any of us or toward their weapons. Though the white lawmen who confronted us were known as being tough, they were under the direction of Chief Harvey, who was just as tough but who remained calm and whose primary goal, as he always told everyone in town, was "keeping things orderly."

We were not surrounded, since the police and the bus were gathered on only one side of the park. Anyone could have run off, and maybe that was Chief Harvey's plan, but no one left. I cannot know what every individual was thinking, but I believe that the young people who were there that day had already decided to face the risk of going to jail. They were there to make a statement. They had come to force their town to change.

Gunter walked over to Chief Harvey and spent a few minutes talking with him. For a while we stood around, getting adjusted to the situation and waiting to see what would happen, until we watched as Gunter was handcuffed and put in one of the police cars. No doubt about it, Gunter had just been arrested. The mood was changing fast. Chief Harvey took a bullhorn out of the same police car.

"Y'all under arrest. You colored kids get in that bus."

The Black students were arrested, taken one at a time to the school bus by the sometimes rough hand of the city police. No one was hit, but these were not gentle arrests. The police took each student by the arm and marched each one to the steps of the bus, to be handed over to another white man with a badge. In this small town the police often knew the student or someone in the student's family, and that might lead to different treatment. From where I stood the police looked like they were being rougher with some of the guys. It took them quite a while to fill the bus.

As the students were being arrested a white man in uniform came over to me and told me to put my hands behind my back. "You ready for jail, nigger-lover? You're under arrest," he said. "Turn around and put your hands behind your back." There was no reason to resist or be difficult. The man put me in handcuffs, the metal kind that use a key. The cuffs were very uncomfortable, but at least the metal didn't cut into my skin. I was grabbed by the arm and pushed over to one of the police cars. Luther had been taken to the bus, along with all the students. Our integrated group was segregated by the police from the moment of our arrest.

Alan and Timothy were being arrested for the first time. Timothy was pacing before his arrest and seemed to be deep in thought. Anticipating jail in Mississippi was scary. He and Alan were arrested one at a time, Alan first, handcuffed and taken to the police cars and put in with Gunter. Timothy was grabbed and put in with me.

There wasn't much conversation in the police car. I never got comfortable sitting on the metal handcuffs, which were digging into my back. I just tried to get as comfortable as possible to handle the pain. Officer Barton was driving and didn't seem to be of a mind to be conversational. That was fine with me. Timothy seemed to still be absorbed in his thoughts.

We were all driven to the county jail on McAdams Street in Kosciusko, just one block from the town square. Set back on a rising hill, the jail was

Fire at the Freedom House

made of brick and had a few small windows blocked by metal bars. Some portions of the brick walls were completely covered by stucco. Sitting on top of a small hill made this one-story lockup look more imposing. It had a front entrance and cell blocks in the back. There was a wide steep driveway for police vehicles. A married police officer had been assigned to live next to the jail, so there was always someone available in an emergency.

Booking us all took some time. I knew the routine – identification, photographs (front and side), fingerprinting and confiscation of personal items that might be used as weapons, wallet and money taken and held "for safekeeping." I didn't feel the need to be a smart-ass this time. I didn't give the police any trouble while they were fingerprinting me. At last the handcuffs were taken off my wrists.

The previous time I was arrested I'd simply been kept sitting in the booking area for a few hours. Once during that time I had been put alone in the drunk tank for about ten minutes. Nothing had happened, so that seemed more like a warning. This time was different. This time I was taken to an area I had never seen before, at the far end of the jail.

I was taken by the arm past a series of cells. I did not know the name of the jailor leading me down the row, but he was not gentle. He forced me along by squeezing tightly into my elbow. There was a musty odor in the cement corridor, with each cell adding its own whiff of human sweat or excrement.

As I was led past the cells I looked at each one. Barren cement rooms with small beds and a toilet behind a solid grill of metal bars. Most were empty. I thought about asking the jailor where we were going, but his fingers in my elbow made me choose silence. Some of the cells were already occupied, all with white men. There were no friendly glances from the prisoners. I was in the white cellblock.

At the end of the row the jailor found the place he had chosen to put me. While keeping his grip on my arm, he reached for his keys and unlocked the dead bolt that made the cell a prison. He swung open the metal door. It was a large cell, with three bunk beds and a toilet. It already held two prisoners. Two white men. Strangers.

"Got you some company, fellas," the jailor said to the men in the cell as he pushed me in. He locked the door behind me.

The two white men were young, in their twenties or thirties. Both had on dungarees and blue short-sleeve shirts. One was taller with a thick head of dark hair. The other was shorter but he had more muscles and a sour expression that made him look menacing. Both men had rough hands and toughened skin.

This was a moment of great fear. I was alone with two white men in a cell about as far away as possible from anyone else. I was sure my luck had run out. These guys were going to pound on me, beat me to a pulp. Every civil rights worker who ever went to jail alone in the Deep South dreaded this moment, a moment without any protection, when old scores could be settled, pent-up anger released, a debt paid back to the jailor or a favor done now for a favor down the road, the beating as certain as the lynching once the rope is around your neck.

I eyed my cellmates, nodded, and sat on a bottom bunk as far away from them as possible. We looked at each other. I was silent. They were sitting on the bottom of the bunk bed on the opposite wall, a hand of cards dealt out between them. No one said a word. I waited and watched for any movement in my direction.

The silence was broken when both Alan and Tim were led into the same cell. "Hey, good to see you guys," I said with both relief and excitement. I was thrilled to see them. Alan was loose, relaxed, and happy to see me, but not nearly as happy as I was to see him. Timothy was quiet, but his presence in the cell tipped the balance of power, three to two. We were glad that the three of us were together.

Perhaps my luck had held. Perhaps this was not my day for a beating.

Our two cellmates no longer seemed so threatening. Timothy appeared to have come to some internal resolution and now seemed to be the most relaxed of all of us. He had the nerve to go over and introduce himself.

"Hi, my name's Tim. They just arrested a whole group of us."

Our cellmates gave him a hard look. One of them talked to him.

"That so? What for?"

"We went over to the park with some of the local Black kids. We were in the teen center and we all got arrested."

"Say what? You one of them Northern agitators."

"Yeah, I guess so. I guess that's what I am."

Just then the police started bringing the Black students into the jail from the school bus. The students were taken to an entirely different part of the jail, separated from us on the basis of skin color and from each other on the basis of gender. While we had been quiet in this cell of white men, the Black students, once they were in the cell block in sufficient numbers, were not quiet at all. While the guys started banging on the bars of the cells, it was the young women who started the singing.

At first it was just a faint chorus off in the distance, but as the number of people put in the cells increased, the chorus grew. A moment of decision had reached our cell. Were we joining in or remaining silent? The singing was infectious. So was the banging on the cell bars and the general ruckus being created. We didn't resist joining in. Banging as loudly on the cells bars as we possibly could, we added to the chaos, joining in the songs when we knew the words. Soon the three of us were caught up in the chorus.

Ain't afraid of your jail
Cause I want my freedom
I want my freedom
I want my freedom
Ain't afraid of your jail
Cause I want my freedom
I want my freedom now!

I felt a wave of joy as we seemed to take control of the small jailhouse. We were locked in our separate cells, but we were joined together in song and the sheer thrill of stirring up a commotion. It was a release from the tension and fear we had all felt from the moment the police had arrived at Jason Niles Park. The singing and the commotion freed us, not from the jail, but from the fear which had bound us since the moment when the police had arrived at the park.

Our cellmates had most likely been bored long before our arrival. They were delighted with the uproar. They didn't seem to care that we were Northern agitators or even what we were up to or why we were arrested. They'd been arrested too, and had been sitting around doing nothing. What they liked now was the riotous atmosphere that the jailors could not control. When it finally quieted down, they became friendly. One of them asked if we had any cigarettes.

"I've got rolling papers and tobacco," said Alan, offering Bugler tobacco around the cell. "I got matches, too." Everyone enjoyed a smoke.

"You guys play Tonk?" one of the men asked. Tonk is a card game I had already learned in the South. It's a cross between gin rummy and poker and has a three-card version as well as a five-card version. Tonk is what the white guys had been playing before we arrived, and it can get boring with only two players. Alan and Tim were quick learners, and within ten minutes we had a lively game. Less than an hour earlier I had been anticipating a brutal stomping from these guys. Now I felt safe.

Unknown to us at the time, the city police were slowly releasing the Black students to their parents, regardless of age. Though some were over 18, like Luther, none of them were held on bond. In conversations later related to us privately by City Attorney Aaron Condon, a decision had been made to hold only the white Northerners for trial. I didn't know where they had taken Gunter, but I assumed he was in another part of the jail. The four of us would be held until we could post bail. We settled in. The idea of a hunger strike never entered my mind. When a dinner of stew and bread and some tea was brought to us, we were happy to eat.

It didn't take long until most of the town knew we had been arrested. While local MFDP members worked on networking with the parents, Betty had been contacting Jackson and getting some lawyers up to Kosciusko. She also worked on getting bail. Gunter must have gotten out first. Before it was dark I was brought to the front and told to sign a city court bond or "recognizance" for $300, secured by Allen Kern, of Kern's Barber Shop, and Irene Smith. The bond was then signed by Judge Roy Mikell, who was to be our trial judge, and I was released. Alan and Tim were out soon after my release. Betty was there to pick us up.

It felt euphoric to be out of jail in the daylight. I had dreaded the possibility of spending the night in jail, or of being released into the darkness. Now I knew all of us were out.

This was the first mass arrest in the history of Kosciusko, and the local people arrested were the children of the Black community. There was a sense of outrage no one had anticipated. This was now about children, a son or a daughter, a niece or a nephew, a grandchild. In the way that the local community was a network of extended families, this was now about everyone's children.

Chapter 20:
Trial at the County Courthouse

On the night of the arrests and in the days that followed there was a buzz of conversation all over town. Many people in the white community were angry, convinced that "outside agitators" were the cause of the problem. A few, however, called the Freedom House and said privately that a pool for only white people was unfair. Many Black adults were angry about the arrests and wanted to do something to support the movement, while others worried that events were happening too quickly and would stir up retribution.

The *Star-Herald* headlined the story of the arrests, the first time it carried news on the local civil rights movement:

> *23 Arrested For Break-in At Pavilion*
>
> Police arrested 23 persons, mostly Negro youngsters, Wednesday afternoon on charges they broke into a locked pavilion at the Kosciusko city park.
>
> Nineteen juveniles in the group were released to their parents pending youth court hearings and four white adults were charged with trespassing.
>
> The four adults arrested were being released on bond.
>
> A group has been picketing occasionally in protest of the lack of swimming facilities here.

The press and the police continued to tell the story as if it was about local teenagers and outside adults, but the reality was that all of us arrested at the park were teenagers, with the single exception of Gunter. Timothy, Luther and others from Tipton were 18, Alan and I were 19. Gunter was the old man at 24. Framing the events as involving "juveniles" and "adults" was code for separating Black from white.

Each of the local Black "juveniles" arrested had a conversation at home. There was strong support for the young people from most parents, but there were households with conflicting emotions and some where the parents did not support what their children had done. MFDP activists started talking about having a Freedom March to show community support for everyone who had been arrested.

I thought of myself as an adult and the law was treating me as an adult, but I also needed to have a conversation with my parents. The only way to get Allen Kern and Irene Smith free of my bond was to come up with $300 in cash. This required a call to my parents in Valley Stream.

"Will you accept a collect call from Matt?" the operator asked.

"Yes, of course," I heard my father say.

"Hi, Dad. We got arrested yesterday trying to integrate the swimming pool. I need to..."

"Wait a second. Let me get your mother on the extension."

"Arrested? What happened?" I heard my mother's voice ask, trying to conceal her panic.

"Nothing," I replied. "Some of us were arrested for trying to integrate the city swimming pool, and I need to reimburse the people who bailed me out of jail. Not a big deal."

"Were you hurt?"

"No."

"Was anyone hurt?"

"No."

"Do you need us to fly down there?"

"Oh, no, please don't. I just need $300 to reimburse the people who put up my bail money."

It took some explaining, since my parents were surprised to learn that we were arrested for being in an empty teen center, but once they understood that the park was open to whites only, it was clear. They were supportive and very relieved there was no violence. My father wired $300 by Western Union. The money went from my hands to the clerk of the court.

Gunter drove me to thank Alan Kern and Irene Smith. I was deeply grateful for what they had done and thanked them profusely for risking their own money to get me out of jail. They were gracious and thanked us for the work we were doing.

There was now a steady stream of visitors to the Freedom House. We started having almost daily visits from young Black men who had gone north to work in the auto industry, mostly in Detroit, and who were back in town on vacation. Many arrived with new cars which were rolling advertisements for migrating North. They had heard that the civil rights movement had arrived in Kosciusko and they dropped by to see for themselves. These young men had been earning a decent wage and many happily peeled off a few bills as a donation. Neighbors brought more food, Roxie Meredith brought more pecan pies, and high school students stopped over to hang out with each other.

The trial came almost immediately. We had all been arrested on Wednesday and four of us went to trial just six days later, on Tuesday afternoon, August 9. The four defendants were Gunter, Alan, Timothy and me, the four white Northerners. The trial was held on the second floor of the Attala County Courthouse in the center of the town square.

I met our lawyer, Kevin Carey, and his chief investigator, Roy Self, for the first time on the day of trial. That summer the legal side of the civil rights movement in Mississippi was still well organized. Betty's call to the Lawyers' Committee for Civil Rights Under Law, which had staff, volunteers, money and offices in Jackson and in Washington, D.C., brought real help. While there were apparently political battles going on among the lawyers, I knew nothing about it at the time and the conflicts didn't seem to impact us. The Lawyers' Committee had gotten both Kevin Carey and Roy Self to Kosciusko by 5 p.m. on the day of the arrests. They conducted their own inspection of Jason Niles Park and the teen center while most of us were still in jail.

We arrived for trial in the best clothes we had with us, which simply meant clean pants and clean shirts. It was my first time inside the courthouse, a striking three-story red brick building with four white columns at the entrance, white trim and a dome with a clock tower at the top. It was built from a design by Andrew J. Bryan in 1897. Bryan traveled the Deep South at the turn of the century constructing magnificent courthouses in Southern town squares.

I had been through the town square almost every day since I had arrived in Kosciusko. I always found my eyes drawn to the courthouse. As we ascended the grand stone staircase at the front entrance on the first day of trial, I looked to my left and saw the monument to Confederate soldiers on the front lawn, added in 1911. It was iconic in Mississippi, a white stone base with a single soldier standing at the top, and looked very much like the statue to the Confederacy we had seen in the Neshoba County town square. One side of the base was engraved, "Attala County's Tribute to Our Boys in Grey: Our Heroes." This was not auspicious.

Once we entered the courthouse we climbed the dark wooden staircase to the second floor and, guided by our lawyer, entered the courtroom. It had beautiful wood-paneled walls complementing an ornate judge's bench, the elevated desk that provides the judge with a view of the entire courtroom. The wood was polished to a glossy shine. We took our seats at the defendant's table.

The prosecuting attorney was George J. Thornton of the local law firm of Thornton and Lindsay.

"All rise before this honorable court of the County of Attala, State of Mississippi."

Judge Ray S. Mikell presiding, he entered from his chambers, a somber man in his forties with a full head of hair and piercing eyes which left no doubt about who was in control.

"Be seated."

The charge was malicious mischief. The allegation was that we had engaged as a group in mischief which had caused property damage in violation of section 2281 of the Mississippi criminal code. While I sat very much in awe of the beauty and solemnity of the setting and the seriousness of the lawyers and the court staff, it was the power radiating from Judge Mikell that drew my attention. His black robe and serious demeanor reminded me this was a real trial with our freedom at stake.

The first witness called by the prosecution was one of the arresting officers.

"Were you present at Jason Niles Park last Wednesday around noon?"

"I was."

"When you arrived at the park, did you have the opportunity to inspect the teen center?"

"I looked at the place. There were a bunch of colored kids and those white fellas over there," he said, gesturing at the defense table.

"Did you have a chance to look at the condition of the teen center?"

"Yes, I did."

"Did you see any damage?"

"Yes, sir. They busted out a window to break into the place. There was glass all over the floor. It was a mess."

"Has that window been fixed yet?

"Nope, not yet. Takes time."

What broken window, I wondered to myself.

A second Kosciusko policeman testified the same way.

"Did you see any damage at the Dixie Pavilion?"

"Yes, sir. One of the windows was broken so those people could get into the Pavilion."

I thought we had broken the law just by bending the screen and entering the teen center. I didn't understand any reason to embellish the story with broken glass, but maybe the police wanted to make the story more dramatic.

Kevin Carey, who had recently come to Mississippi from the state of Oregon, seemed genuinely surprised that policemen would lie under oath. He tried to shake their testimony on cross-examination, but the officers were unflappable. The prosecution rested its case.

Mr. Carey then put on Roy Self. The investigator testified that he had inspected the teen center at Jason Niles Park around 5 p.m. on the day of the arrests. He stated that no windows were broken at that time and no broken glass was evident on the floor. He also testified that he had visited the building again before coming to the courthouse that day and again none of the windows were broken.

The prosecution had a few questions.

"Are you from Attala County, Mr. Self?"

"No, sir."

"You come up here from Jackson?"

"Yes, sir."

"You come up here with that Lawyers' Committee for Civil Rights?"

"Objection, your honor. Lacks relevance."

"Your honor, of course it's relevant. Goes to bias."

"Objection overruled. I want to hear the answer."

"So again, Mr. Self, did you come up here paid for by the Lawyers' Committee for Civil Rights?"

"Yes, sir."

"Nothing further, your honor."

"Mr. Self," Kevin Carey got to ask, "Did the fact that you were hired out of Jackson affect your ability to see if any windows were broken at the teen center last Wednesday?"

"No, sir, not at all."

"Or today?"

"No, sir."

"Were there any broken windows at the teen center on the day you first inspected the teen center?"

"No."

"Were there any broken windows today?"

"No, sir."

"Nothing further, your honor."

And that was it. This was a trial without a transcript and without a jury. I doubt a jury would have made any difference.

Judge Mikell left the bench for about five minutes. When he returned the court was called back to order.

The judge fixed us with a stare. "This court finds all four defendants guilty of malicious mischief, as charged. I sentence each one of you to 90 days in jail and a fine of ten dollars." He pounded the gavel.

Ninety days in a Mississippi jail. I had never expected such a sentence. While our lawyer was still upset about the testimony of the policemen, I was upset by the 90-day sentence. Where would we serve the time? How would we be treated? Ninety days and nights in a cell as a civil rights worker seemed likely to be hard time. At least we knew in advance that, if we were sentenced to jail time, we would not be taken away that day. Instead the lawyers went up to the bench and, after a consultation with the judge, Mr. Carey formally appealed the verdict. We were entitled to a trial "de novo" in the Circuit Court, which meant a new, second trial on the same charge.

We were told later that Judge Mikell conceded in chambers, after the trial, that the evidence as to the window was "inconclusive," but he told the lawyers that he found that someone in our group must have bent the screen, even though no evidence about the screen had been submitted and the damage to the screen, if any, "was too small to be measured." For

Judge Mikell, it seemed our entry into Jason Niles Park was enough for a guilty verdict.

What the Judge did with the bail was the real message. He lowered the appeal bail to $150, refunding $150 to each of us. As Kevin Carey told the story, he asked the judge why bail was being lowered after his clients had been convicted. Judge Mikell apparently responded, "You know, Mr. Carey, a lower bail just might make it easier for these defendants to leave town without appearing for a new trial."

That may have been Judge Mikell's plan. It was not our plan.

FREEDOM MARCH

PLACE – CHRISTIAN LIBERTY
            2ND BAPTIST CHURCH
DATE – SATURDAY – AUGUST 13th
TIME – 2:00 P.M.

IF there ARE MANY PEOPLE
ON THE MARCH — IT MEANS POWER.
IF THERE ARE ONLY A FEW —
IT MEANS NOTHING. So PLEASE
COME AND JOIN THE MARCH.
AND GIVE THE CIVIL RIGHTS
MOVEMENT POWER

THERE WILL BE NO ARRESTS!

JOIN THE
            FREEDOM MARCH

MFDP leaflet, Kosciusko, August 1966.

Chapter 21:
Freedom March in Kosciusko

The arrests of the most militant students at Tipton High for trying to use Jason Niles Park triggered community outrage and a protective emotion that generated the momentum for a Freedom March. The MFDP had talked about the possibility of a march earlier in the summer, when Lawrence Guyot spoke at the Wesley Methodist Church in July. The idea now spread swiftly.

Open proponents for white supremacy in those times often portrayed Mississippi Blacks as satisfied. "Our coloreds are happy with the way things are" would be the polite way this idea was expressed. Often more offensive language was used. This notion was widespread in the white community. It was self-deception.

Immediately after the arrests, local MFDP activists started planning for a Freedom March on Saturday, August 13.

In the Black community, these two words, Freedom and March, were each powerful. When joined together, embodying both the goal and the drive of the civil rights movement, they were audacious. This was bold language in any town in Mississippi in the sixties.

A Freedom March in Kosciusko would be a challenge to the white community. A march would be a demand for racial equality and an end to the brutality of white supremacy. A march would be the Black community speaking loudly through the physical act of walking together as a group, to the county courthouse, on a Saturday afternoon, when the town square would typically be filled with people.

One measure of a successful march would be the number and variety of people who participated. People looked around and showed themselves to each other on a Freedom March in a small town. Many individuals had registered to vote, or had been to a civil rights meeting. Showing oneself in public was another matter. The march, if effective, would allow the local Black community to see its own strength.

Organizing for the march required the participation of the churches, which were the only spaces where Black people could gather in large numbers. The MFDP had been meeting regularly at Wesley Methodist Church with the cooperation of Rev. B.F. Harper, a solid voice in support of the movement. Beatrice and Elmore Winfrey were Baptists, the Mallets were part of Buffalo United Methodist and the Meredith family belonged to Wesley Methodist.

There was a significant Black Baptist congregation in the city and the rural Black community was overwhelmingly Baptist. Christian Liberty Baptist Church in Kosciusko stepped forward, as did the Baptist congregation in Sallis and the White Plains Baptist Church in McCool. To build unity, the MFDP held the planning meeting for the march at Wesley Methodist, while the Freedom March itself on Saturday was scheduled to begin with a meeting at Christian Liberty Baptist on South Tipton.

We printed hundreds of leaflets to publicize the planning meeting on Thursday. The leaflet was the first to convey a sense of urgency.

CIVIL RIGHTS MEETING
Place - Wesley Methodist Church
Date - Thursday, August 11th
Time - 8:00 P.M.

LET'S TALK ABOUT:
1. Recent Arrests of Many Negro Teenagers
2. Parks and Swimming Pool
3. School Integration
4. The March
5. School Union
6. *Jobs in the Stores and Banks*
If you have never been to a civil rights meeting before, COME NOW! If you have come before, COME AGAIN! Don't stay home and watch TV, or go to Durant, or be too busy to come. We need EVERYONE to make this civil rights fight work.

Come to the Meeting!
FREEDOM NOW

The high school students who had been arrested walked door to door in the city with the leaflets, while those who could drive helped spread the news throughout the county. Alan and Timothy continued house visits with local MFDP activists. In addition to going to homes, we brought leaflets to Black-owned businesses throughout town, including the Dixie Café, Bell's Pool Hall and all the Black barbershops. Betty brought leaflets to the Black beauty salons. We tried to cover all the small grocery stores and fix-it shops that some people operated out of their homes.

"You think folks will turn out for this march?" asked Izah Brown, when I brought a small pile of leaflets to his store.

"Mr. Brown," I replied, "as best as I can tell, there's a lot of people planning to be there."

"Matt, you know people don't always do what they say. I don't have to school you on that, do I?"

"Oh, I understand, really I do. But people have been doing a tremendous amount, and it just feels like this is the time to bring everybody together." I was being sincere. The mood in town was different. There was a shared sense that what the police had done had crossed the line.

A month earlier we had printed the leaflet for the July MFDP meeting on a cheap stencil, with money Gunter cajoled from my diminishing stash. Now donations came in every day, some of it from the young auto workers, some of it money donated at meetings and some sent from up north by relatives and friends of the youth who had been arrested. We were able to pay all of our accumulated bills for auto repair, purchase car parts and oil and even buy new tires for the car.

Now we printed all the leaflets on a small mimeograph machine sent to us from Jackson. The only alternative at the time, a printing press, was far too expensive. The mimeo, as it was called, required a sharp blade to cut a stencil, which was then placed on a small rotating drum filled with a foul-smelling ink. Turning a hand crank forced ink through the openings in the stencil, printing a leaflet on each sheet of paper fed into the machine. We were done when the stencil ripped, which happened often with cheap stencils. Now we could buy quality stencils and all the ink and paper we needed. We cranked away.

It helped tremendously to have Alan and Timothy on the team. They brought a huge increase in the energy we could devote to distributing leaflets. Activists went door to door throughout the community.

The organizing for the Freedom March was bringing out people in unprecedented numbers. There was a large turnout for the meeting on Thursday night. I spent that night guarding the Freedom House, but Alan said he counted well over 100 people at the meeting. I was also told that part of the discussion concerned rumors that the high school students would be put on probation for two years, a threat meant to discourage future activism. This was unacceptable.

It may have taken the intervention of Dock Drummond for the white political leadership to see that any more trouble for the high school students would provoke a unified community response. Aaron Condon called the Freedom House late Thursday night and told us that both Mayor Doty Jackson and Chief of Police Harvey had spoken with Dock Drummond, had agreed to drop the threat of probation and agreed the march would be allowed to proceed. The MFDP won a guarantee that there would be no arrests of participants in the march. This was made so clear that we were able to state it publicly.

Soon we had hundreds of leaflets to distribute which announced:

FREEDOM MARCH
Place - Christian Liberty
2nd Baptist Church
Date - Saturday - August 13th
Time – 2:00 P.M.

If there are many people on the March – it means power. If there are only a few – it means nothing. So please come and JOIN THE MARCH and give the civil rights movement POWER.
THERE WILL BE NO ARRESTS!

JOIN THE
FREEDOM MARCH

The ability to state there would be no arrests of participants in the march meant more than just no arrests. It meant that we had been told by the white power structure that it would not provoke or allow conflict. It was as much an assurance to the Black community as it was a warning to elements in the white community who might think about causing trouble.

We became confident that there would be at least 200 people on the march. In our exuberance we asked the Jackson office to print bumper stickers saying FREEDOM NOW, for which we would pay. A bundle of bright orange bumper stickers promptly arrived, proclaiming in bold black letters, FREEDOM NOW, and beneath that in smaller letters, ATTALA COUNTY FREEDOM MOVEMENT. It was immediately obvious this was a mistake. Why would anyone put one on their car or truck? Why invite slashed tires or worse? I never saw a single bumper sticker on a single car. The bumper stickers at least got put to use as small signs carried on the march.

On the afternoon of August 13 over 200 people gathered outside the Christian Liberty Baptist Church. The high school students were there with their families and friends. Dock Drummond, Susie Bell and J.P. Presley participated, as did Albert Truss, Allen Kern, Irene Smith, Shirley Adams, Nash Hannah and Mike Bell. Elmore and Beatrice Winfrey were there, as were all the Malletts, including Lenora Mallett. Kevin Carey was there, having driven up from Jackson for the day.

This was the Freedom March we had all worked so hard to create. There was a brief service at the church, after which the marchers gathered on the street, with monitors from the MFDP. Some people joined us along the route as we marched up Tipton Street past houses and shacks. As we reached the town square area and marched past single-story shops and stores, there was no harassment from the few white people on the sidewalks. The mood was calm and determined.

Members of the choirs from the Wesley Methodist and Christian Liberty congregations led singing that reflected the mood. The most memorable to me was "Oh, Freedom," a responsive song that allowed a choir member to call out a line the crowd could quickly learn. Using a bullhorn, a choir member led the first stanza:

> *Oh, freedom, oh, freedom*
> *Oh, freedom over me, over me*
> *And before I'll be a slave*
> *I'll be buried in my grave*
> *And go home to my Lord and be free*

The Choir leader called out, "No segregation!" and the marchers responded:

No segregation, no segregation
No segregation over me, over me
And before I'll be a slave
I'll be buried in my grave
And go home to my Lord and be free.
Choir leader, "No more lynchings!"

No more lynchings, no more lynchings
No more lynchings over me, over me
And before I'll be a slave
I'll be buried in my grave
And go home to my Lord and be free.

As we marched, Luther and I stayed together and watched the streets and rooftops. Despite the desire of the white power structure to avoid an incident and stay out of the news, and despite the pressure being exerted by Chief Harvey, there was always the possibility that some white man would take it upon himself to attack us.

"Looks pretty safe to me," I said at one point.

"This is Mississippi," Luther responded quickly. "You best keep your eyes open."

When we reached the town square there were more Black people waiting for us near the courthouse steps. At least 50 more people joined the Freedom March at that point, including Pearl Nash, Edgar Nash and Roxie Meredith, people who had not walked with the group but wanted to be present for the public rally. By this time our numbers had swelled to over 300, enough to make a deep impression on the county. A few dozen white people lined the sidewalks of the town square, but there was no taunting and no jeering. The city police kept watch from three or four vantage points. It seemed to me there was a quiet sense of wonderment.

We held a rally on the southeast side of the courthouse, our backs turned on the monument to the Confederacy. Ironically, the statue of the Confederate soldier atop the monument had his back turned on us.

Dock Drummond and Susie Bell spoke, as did Rev. B.F. Harper and Rev. Ash and a group of the high school students. Kevin Carey was asked to say a few words about people's legal rights. We ended with "We Shall Overcome."

As we marched out of the square there was a sense of elation among us. This had been a huge moment for people, an event few thought they would ever see in Kosciusko. All our effort felt validated. There was a power in our numbers, and there was power in the fact that the Freedom March had been peaceful. As we left the square and passed the pool hall, one man stepped off, leaned against a wall and announced over and over again to all who would listen, "I am a man! I told you, I am a man!"

Luther at the Kosciusko Freedom House.
Photo by the author

Chapter 22:
Two Packs of No-Doz

Luther and I were eager to set up a Freedom House somewhere in McCool, and we knew that the addition of Alan and Timothy as full-time staff had given us the opportunity to expand our reach. But suddenly it seemed that Timothy might leave.

In their first days in Kosciusko, Alan and Timothy had been arrested, put on trial, convicted and sentenced to 90 days in jail. Alan still said he felt nurtured in Attala County, compared to the isolation he had felt in Ferriday. We knew we could count on him.

Timothy was having a more difficult time. Events had happened so fast it was unnerving him. Unfamiliar with the local roads, a few days after the mass arrest he crashed a borrowed truck into a utility pole on Boyd Street. Timothy had arrived from New Jersey with a small stash of money. He had already covered his travel expenses and his bail money, and now he paid for the truck repairs out of his own pocket.

But money did not seem to be the problem. Timothy started talking about the possibility that he might not be ready for the risks we were taking. He had been calm and marvelous in jail, but the prospect of a 90-day sentence began to haunt him. We wondered if he would stay.

If we were to expand to McCool, we needed a full staff back in Kosciusko. We also needed a house. In the midst of organizing for the march, we started to push Gunter to come through on a vague comment he had made about a shack we could use.

"Hey Gunter," Luther said one morning, "Whatever happened to that house you know about outside McCool? You talk to anybody about it?"

"Yeah, not yet. I will when I can get around to it," was Gunter's response. Sometimes it was difficult to know what he was really thinking.

Yet the day after the march, Gunter told me we needed to visit someone, and I got in the car. It was a typical road trip with him. We were going somewhere, but I didn't know where. So far it had always worked out well. We would often travel to visit someone who was a stranger to me but who knew Gunter, and the person would help us in some way, like the man who had led us through the forest during the gunfight in Neshoba County. This time I tried to write down the directions. My cryptic note reads:

"Natchez Trace, 10 miles before Canton, on left, 4 H Club, next house."

That was it. We traveled the Natchez Trace south, then turned west toward Canton. The "next house" belonged to a Black woman who appeared to be in her forties. She was friendly but seemed nervous. She did not invite us inside. She and Gunter spoke privately on the side of her home while I waited.

When we got back in the car Gunter had the key to a house in McCool. We drove back to Kosciusko, picked up Luther and headed to see the shack that Gunter had talked about for weeks.

At the turnoff to McCool, a tributary of the Yockanookany ran between the highway and the downtown buildings. We had driven over a small bridge the first time we went to McCool and entered Bowie's Grocery and Café. We crossed that bridge again to visit the building that might become our new Freedom House.

The shack sat on a plot of land in a predominantly Black neighborhood in the woods south of town, an area where small houses were connected by dirt roads. The shack was made of thin pine boards and tar paper, only the brick and mortar chimney having any substance. Some of the windows were broken. The place looked like it had been abandoned for years, with debris cluttering the floor.

"Hey, Gunter," said Luther after a brief inspection. "Are you serious? This is one sorry house."

Gunter just shrugged. "It's the best we could do. You two can always go over to Nash's place."

"What do you think of this?" Luther directed at me.

"Well, at least it's not camping," I said. "It's a house, not a tent. You okay with it?"

We looked the place over. The shack was on a dirt road across from an open field, set in the midst of a lightly wooded forest. A large area was cleared of brush, making it easy to park. The house had no running water,

Fire at the Freedom House

but we could deal with that. At least there was an outhouse set back in the trees. It would do.

At one point a pickup truck with two white men in overalls drove by on the dirt road. The man in the passenger seat gave us a long stare.

We needed to look around more. We explored outside. I followed a short path through the trees in back of the house and came to an empty church facing another dirt road. The building was well maintained and looked like it was still holding services. It was helpful to know there was a back exit if we ever needed to make a quick retreat.

Another truck drove by, driven by a Black man in overalls. He glanced at us and kept driving.

Gunter and Luther visited three houses down the road. All were occupied by Black people. One adult man had been cautiously welcoming. He said that farmers regularly used the dirt road we were on.

We decided the location was worth a try. We would turn the shack into a new Freedom House.

Luther and I made a list of what we needed to bring from Kosciusko. Written on a scrap of paper on our way back to town, it reads:

> kerosene lamp, lamp globe (2 lamps?)
>
> mattress, blankets
>
> 2 packages NO-DOZ
>
> 1 water jug
>
> toilet paper
>
> cigarettes
>
> cotton
>
> newspaper (for under mattress)
>
> posters, signs
>
> 2 pistols, 2 shotguns
>
> two chairs
>
> radio
>
> flashlight
>
> locks

That first visit was on a Sunday, and it was mostly a day of rest. We came back to Kosciusko in the early afternoon. Most stores were closed, and Luther and I had no interest in gathering up our list of items. We could do it all tomorrow. I was interested in getting some food, and I think Luther may have gone to visit another girlfriend.

We came back to the news that Timothy was leaving. He had decided to go, and he already had a ride to the Jackson airport. Leaving meant jumping bail on the conviction for malicious mischief, but that was fine, since it also meant avoiding the 90-day jail sentence. I was sorry to see him leave. I still felt grateful for how he had changed the mood in the jail cell when we were all arrested, but I had to assume he was making the right decision for himself. He left before dark.

Alan would be staying in Kosciusko without Timothy, but he was relieved to be working with Betty and Gunter after his difficulties in Ferriday. He repeated that he felt welcomed in the community.

Would Luther and I still try to establish a Freedom House in McCool? We all felt it could be done.

The next day, in the early afternoon, Luther and I went to one of the Sunflower Markets to buy food and supplies. There were Black and white customers shopping and we drew no special attention or hostility. We made a stop at Pickle's Drug Store in the town square, probably for the two packages of No-Doz and some bandages for wounds. A white man I took to be Bill Pickle treated us courteously at the counter.

Later that afternoon, Luther and I finally started on our journey to McCool. I drove the truck, our supplies loaded in the back, both of us thinking we would draw less attention if we looked like a white man driving a hired hand. I turned east off Highway 12, crossed the Yockanookany and headed toward the plot of land we had just visited on Sunday.

The house was gone.

The tall brick chimney stood alone in a field of ashes. Fire had completely destroyed the house. There was charred wood and the smell of smoke everywhere. The fire had burned out on the edges of the cleared field. The forest stood as silent witness on three sides of the lot. We stood in shock on the dirt road, facing the burn.

I felt numb. Luther said something like, "They got us good." We walked around the field, the scarred and cracked chimney standing as a monument to the inferno that had consumed everything around it. A few scraps of tar paper littered the ground or hung from the charred branches of trees growing near the shack. Mostly I remember the stench, the total silence, the feeling of desolation and the ash that covered everything.

We didn't stay long. I think we both wanted to get out of there as quickly as possible. I was still numb during the drive back to Kosciusko.

That night the members of the local MFDP steering committee met at a private home to talk about how to respond. The group included Susie Bell, Elmore Winfrey, Dock Drummond and Nash Hannah. This was followed the next day by many small conversations.

News of the fire was talked about among neighbors, in the stores, in the barbershops and in the pool hall. Everybody involved in the movement, or not, had an opinion. Many people just hoped there wouldn't be more trouble. Some people felt that it was foolish and too dangerous to go back to McCool, while others were of the opinion that once a stand had been taken, we shouldn't let them run us out.

It was a very informal method of decision-making. Luther and I spoke with Nash Hannah, who told us we would need to agree if the decision was made to return. "If you do come back," he said, "I'll be there for you one hundred percent."

Somehow a conclusion was reached. We would rebuild the Freedom House. Luther and I were both fine with the decision. Mr. Winfrey was a skilled carpenter and would plan and supervise the building of a cabin. It would be a small solid room with two doors and no windows. There would be rectangular openings that would allow us to see outside. There would still be no water, but the outhouse had not burned. We could handle it.

The cost of the materials would be covered by the donations that had flowed into the movement. Local activists now started speaking about the civil rights efforts in Attala County as "the project" as a way to group together all the steps Black people were taking to end the rule of white supremacy. Rebuilding in McCool was part of the project.

Two days after the fire, we got a phone call from Aaron Condon about our legal problems. He did not have good news. The justice of the peace with jurisdiction over Beat Three, in the northeast corner of Attala County, would be hearing the charges against Gunter for "pointing and aiming a deadly weapon" during the civil rights meeting at the White Plains Baptist Church in McCool in July. The case would be called for hearing on Wednesday.

The news was alarming, but it strengthened our resolve not to be pushed out of McCool. It also required another call to the Lawyers' Committee in Jackson.

On a muggy Wednesday three of us, Gunter, Kevin Carey and I, drove to McCool for Gunter's hearing. Kevin was still our lawyer, and now he was our driver, since we were in his rental car. His air-conditioned rental car. What comfort! Gunter sat in the front and talked, mostly about the case. While they talked, I relaxed in the back seat and enjoyed the cool air and the serene beauty of the countryside.

The hearing was held in a cinderblock back room of a building near Bowie's Café and Grocery. When we pulled into town there were an unusual number of cars and pickup trucks parked on the roadside. It was quiet as Kevin pulled off the road and parked. It was hot, a blast of heat when we got out of the car, and there was no one out on the street.

The cinderblock room was now transformed into a courtroom. A long folding table placed in front of the room became the judge's bench. The Mississippi State flag hung from a pole, the Confederate battle flag in the upper left corner, always a reminder of slavery. Two small tables with chairs faced the judge's table. Folding chairs were set out in the rear. The room was already filled with spectators. White men.

The local justice of the peace sat behind the front table. He was thin, with grey hair and an angular, chiseled face. He wore a black judicial robe. At least 20 white people occupied the folding chairs or stood with their backs to the cinderblock walls. A few glared at us as we made our way to the small table for the defense. The acrid smell of tobacco and sweat filled the room.

Kevin Carey greeted the prosecuting attorney, who was seated at the prosecutor's table and was the only other man in the room wearing a suit and tie. I looked around at the crowd. Most chatted quietly with each other, waiting for justice to be meted out. Some men met my gaze directly, not hesitant to look me in the eye.

Two white men were called by the prosecutor as witnesses. The first witness, a man in his thirties with a round face and dark hair, testified.

"Were you present at the meeting at the White Plains Church in July?"

"No, sir, I wasn't at the meeting. I was just driving by."

"That's okay. And while driving by, did anybody threaten you?"

"Objection, ambiguous, Your Honor," started Mr. Carey.

"Mr. Carey," the justice of the peace cut him off, "we don't accept objections here." The justice then looked over at the witness. "Answer the question."

"Let me ask you this way," the prosecutor continued. "When you were driving by the White Plains Church, did anyone in this room here today point a weapon at you?"

"Well, yes, sir. That fella over there pointed a rifle at me. That tall fuzzy one," he said, nodding at Gunter.

The second witness gave the same testimony.

Gunter was sworn in, and denied pointing a weapon at anyone.

"I was keeping watch for the meeting when cars filled with armed men started driving on the road. I was holding a rifle, but I always kept it pointed at the ground. No one ever pointed a weapon at me, and I never pointed a weapon at anyone."

There was some cross-examination, but by this time I understood from Mr. Carey that the testimony didn't really matter. The justice of the peace could only send the matter on for a trial of record in the Circuit Court, and the outcome of this hearing had been decided before testimony began.

The matter was submitted, with the prosecutor arguing that the matter came down to the credibility of the witnesses and, he said pointedly, it was obvious to everyone in the room who should be believed.

The justice of the peace was ready. "It is ordered that the defendant in this case stand trial before the Circuit Court of the County of Attala on the charges filed." The gavel fell.

There followed some conversation at the front table. It became clear to the spectators that Gunter was not being taken away. The room slowly emptied out, the men talking among themselves as they left. I waited, and thought I heard someone muttering, "He should be dealt with already." They had been there to see justice meted out, and all they had seen were papers being signed. I started worrying that they would be waiting for us outside, chewing on their anger.

After all the paperwork was filled out and signed, we were free to go. When we walked out there were three or four cars still parked on the side of the road. One small cluster of men stood around a pickup truck, staring at us as we walked to the rental car. I stayed alert for any sudden movement. After we were able to drive away, I watched the road behind us for miles. We were not followed.

In the days that followed, we set out to build the McCool Freedom House. The first task was to clear away the pieces of metal, broken glass and strips of tar paper which were strewn among the ashes. Once we had a reasonably clear area, with Mr. Winfrey's direction we started building a simple foundation on cement blocks. This was not much different than many of the shacks in the area. On the foundation we built a wooden floor and a frame for walls. Mr. Winfrey started arriving on a daily basis.

As soon as there was a solid floor above the ashes, Luther and I started spending nights at the site, alternately sleeping and staying awake, guarding our construction. The chimney loomed over us, a constant reminder that we had enemies. Early one evening, while Gunter and Wiley were still at the work site, we had a visit.

Two gun shots rang out in the distance. Startled, a flock of birds took flight and something ran through the forest. As the sound of the shots faded away, the stuttering rumble of two truck engines filled the air. I hadn't seen anything yet, but I grabbed my rifle and took cover behind a tree on the edge of the burned area. Two pickup trucks filled with white men, all of them armed, pulled up on the dirt road in front of us and stopped. I did a quick count and figured four or five men in each truck.

Luther, a pistol in his hand, found cover behind the remains of the chimney. He and I exchanged a quick glance. Wiley crouched behind the edge of our station wagon, reaching for a shotgun in the back seat. Gunter stood alone, facing the pickup trucks, defiant, an open target.

"Hey, what the hell you doing on this land?" demanded one of the men from the back of a truck. "You're a goddamn trespasser."

Gunter took his time answering. He kept one hand on the butt of the pistol sticking out of his right pocket. His height and his brazen attitude kept the attention focused on him. He barely moved.

"Well, somebody burned down this house. You here to apologize?"

I thought they were here to kill us. So far the men in the trucks had their guns pointed in the air or at the ground, but I didn't like the look in their eyes. I glanced at Wiley, who now had the shotgun, and again at Luther. They were both focused on the men in the trucks. Gunter seemed

Fire at the Freedom House

calm and unimpressed by our visitors. I stayed frozen in place, my hands clutching the rifle, my finger on the trigger.

"Apologize? Hell no," responded the man who seemed to be in charge, staring at Gunter. "We're here to deliver a message. Get the hell out of McCool now, while you're still alive."

The scene was unfolding before me in slow motion. Any threatening gesture, any suspicious movement, might unleash a fusillade of gunfire. I thought I might be about to die. But as I looked at the scene, I began to realize that the men confronting us were as vulnerable as Gunter. Standing in the open backs of the pickup trucks, they must have known they were easy targets. A gun battle would not go well for anyone.

Gunter, speaking each word slowly for emphasis, replied with "We're not going anywhere."

"Yeah? Well, then, we'll know just where to find y'all," were the leader's parting words.

As I watched from behind the tree, both pickup trucks took off down the road. They fired two more shots as they left, but not until they were out of sight. Gunter fired one shot in response, not aiming at anything, but trying to show defiance.

Wiley was the first to speak. "I thought I was about to be put to the test," he said. Luther agreed. Though I tried to remain calm, my fear was more intense than ever. I kept it contained within myself. Our message was meant to be clear. We were staying.

We didn't need any No-Doz that night. A little moonshine would have been nice.

The remains of the first Freedom House in McCool.
Photo by the author

Fire at the Freedom House

Chapter 23:
Revival: In the Everlasting Arms

"Good morning. How'd things go last night?"

It was Mr. Winfrey, arriving for another day of work. He was now making the round trip from town every day to work on the construction, often driving by himself, exposed and vulnerable. He seemed to be at peace with the risk he was taking.

"Just fine, Mr. Winfrey, just fine. No problems," Luther replied.

Mr. Winfrey had gathered the lumber and materials in Kosciusko and brought them in stages to McCool. He could rely on a work crew that included Luther and me, Wiley, a few of the high school activists and Alan. There was always someone based in Kosciusko, usually Gunter and Betty, so we could maintain activity and communication in the city at the same time we expanded.

"Mrs. Winfrey packed some food for you. There's some coffee in the thermos."

That was good news. Luther and I didn't have a kitchen or any way to cook. We were living in a partially completed large room which we had the audacity to call a Freedom House. We had a cooler and we had some packaged snacks, but we were being fed mainly by the Nash family and Mrs. Winfrey.

Soon after Luther and I had breakfast, Gunter drove up in the station wagon, bringing with him Wiley and one of the Black high school activists, Tom McAdory. They also brought more food, from Mrs. Mallett and the McAdory family. This was a big work crew for us, and we were all there to work under the direction of Mr. Winfrey.

We unloaded the truck, which was carrying pine boards, roofing material and tools. This was the day we would finish the house. Luther and I would have four walls, a roof, and two doors we could close and lock. While we worked, we listened for approaching cars or trucks, but we had no hostile visits.

I brought no skill in carpentry. Though we had "shop class" for boys in junior high school in Valley Stream, all I had made was a chess board. I couldn't even identify some of the equipment we were using. At one point, Mr. Winfrey needed a tool that had been left in town. He sent Tom to borrow one from a white truck driver who lived within walking distance.

We had met the truck driver through Nash Hannah. This was the white man who drove a big rig and occasionally made runs "up north" to the industrial belt in the Midwest. When Nash introduced us to him, the man said, "It's a different world out there. This system here can't last." It was heartening to hear these sentiments. Still, I wasn't sure what would happen at the man's house.

Mr. Elmore Winfrey preparing
the day's work in McCool.
Photo by the author

Fire at the Freedom House

"How'd it go?" I asked when Tom came back with the tool.

"Okay. More than okay."

"What's that mean? What happened?" asked Luther.

"Well, the man said we could borrow it, and told me where it was in his garage. Thing is, he let me just go in there and pick it out. Didn't even come in the garage with me."

Luther and Wiley understood immediately. It took me a minute. It was extraordinary for a white man to trust a Black person who was not known to him. This simple act was a show of respect.

We finished the construction that day. As a final flourish we painted the words FREEDOM HOUSE in bold black letters above the front door. Luther and I now settled into this remote outpost of the civil rights movement.

We developed a daily routine of canvassing the Black community around McCool, beginning with the people who had already welcomed us, like Tathilia Gaston and the Dotson family. They suggested other people we might visit. We carried voter registration forms. We looked for outgoing people who might network with their family, church and social communities.

Door-to-door canvassing was sometimes considered drudgery, but traveling the back roads of Mississippi was never dull. Luther and I were always vigilant. Any encounter with another vehicle involved mutual scrutiny. If we passed a car or truck with white people in it, we stayed alert to any chance they might chase us. When we spoke with Black people on their porch or in their yard, we kept an eye on our surroundings. I only felt safe when we were invited inside.

Luther did not have a network of family and friends in this part of the county, though he did have one woman he called "Auntie" who lived in the area. We relied on people to suggest other people to contact, and often mentioned Nash Hannah. Most people knew who we were, since the burning of the Freedom House and its rebuilding was big news in a community which had felt secluded from the turmoil of the civil rights movement rolling through the state.

We covered some areas around Ethel, but we never crossed the border into Choctaw County or Winston County, which were only a few miles from us. "Don't ever go to Ackerman," in Choctaw County, was a strict instruction from Gunter. We had no contacts there and no way to know how local law enforcement would react to us. More threatening, we had no way to know how local whites would react to us. We stayed near McCool, encouraging Black adults to register to vote.

The whiskey vote still mattered in Attala, since the issue would likely be on the ballot again in two years. The McCool voting district, which was mostly white, had reported 141 votes against alcohol and only 64 to go wet. There was a heavy evangelical presence in the rural Black community which disdained the use of alcohol, and their votes might help offset the pro-alcohol city vote. This, and a growing sense that Black suffrage was inevitable, may have created some ambivalence among rural whites about our efforts.

Mr. Winfrey working with Tom McAdory, Luther Mallett
and Wiley Mallett to rebuild the Freedom House in McCool.
Photo by the author

Fire at the Freedom House

When the sun set we would generally be back at the Freedom House. We settled into a pattern of doing shifts on guard duty every night, so that we each had a chance to sleep. I would take a No-Doz when Luther went to sleep, which kept me sharp past midnight. Most of the time I was either pacing or sitting in one of the folding chairs, alert to the sounds around me. I spent the first hours with the radio on, catching some rock station that kept playing "Hot Time, Summer in the City." The line "back of my neck getting dirt and gritty" spoke to how I felt all summer. After the early darkness I turned the radio off. Any sound of traffic in the distance demanded that I be focused, listening to the sounds of the night.

When I felt myself getting bleary I would wake up Luther. He was easy to rouse, despite some muttering. Sometimes he would take a No-Doz at 2 a.m. We didn't use it just to stay awake, we used it to wake up. I would sleep on the mattress Luther had just vacated. In the morning he would wake me up and I would take a dose of No-Doz like a shot of morning coffee.

One night, after we had settled into our routine, the forest came alive. First we heard the sound of engines coming through the trees, followed by car doors being opened and closed, the voices of men and women in quiet conversation. A congregation was gathering in the church behind us. As darkness fell, we began to hear the sound of singing coming from the church, muted at first by the trees.

For three nights waves of sound enveloped us. A preacher's voice led the congregation in spiraling rounds of song. I was soothed by the sounds of what, Luther explained to me, was an evangelical revival. The preacher's voice called forth fervor in response, and we thought that during the revival more than a few souls were saved. We were treated to shouting, hand clapping, foot stomping versions of many traditional gospel hymns. "Leaning On the Everlasting Arms" was particularly soothing:

Oh, what a fellowship, what a joy divine,
Leaning on the everlasting arms;
Oh, what a blessedness, what a peace is mine,
Leaning on the everlasting arms.

Leaning, leaning,
Safe and secure from all alarms;
Leaning, leaning,
Leaning on the everlasting arms.

Oh, what have I to dread, what have I to fear,
Leaning on the everlasting arms;
Oh, I have blessed peace with my Lord so near,
Leaning on the everlasting arms.

On the nights of the revival I felt "safe and secure from all alarms." I did not think night riders would attack us while a congregation was worshipping, despite the horror of the Birmingham church bombing three years earlier. I felt comforted by the revival, rousing as it could be, as though the spiritual power being released somehow sheltered us.

Early in this period we learned that Betty had gone back to Vicksburg. I never understood all the reasons she traveled between Kosciusko and Vicksburg. She wrote to me in late August, sending the letter to me at the Winfrey home. Mr. Winfrey brought it to me on one of his trips to McCool, bringing us more food.

Dear Matt,

I thought about writing to Mrs. Winfrey in the first place, but I didn't know the address. Sorry about Gunter. I'm sure you understand the situation now.

How's the office in McCool progressing? I really admire Nash Hannah. I just hope nothing will happen to any of you out there. Are you just going to work in McCool or the other neighboring communities too?

I miss you all, do take care of yourselves and write when you feel up to it and keep me informed on what's going on in McCool.

I saw Gunter. He came through here Sat. Take care and tell Luther hello for me.

Love,

Betty

I never understood the relationship between Betty and Gunter. There must have been a drama unfolding between them, but I had no insight about it. What I did understand was that Betty was gone, and I missed her.

She had left in the past and had always returned. Over time she had told me about working with CORE in other areas of Mississippi. I learned from her that many organizers in the Deep South often did not stay long in a single location. She was prescient when she said in June that we were expendable. She was strong in her belief that those of us at the Freedom House were catalysts, not leadership. There could only be success if a local movement was built.

The draft, which faced all young men in the movement, was an additional risk to our small group. It was no secret that Alan and I were leaving sometime in September to go back to college, unless we wound up back in jail first. Luther had no college plans and was already anticipating being called for a draft physical.

By 1966 the draft for the war in Vietnam was a grim reaper. John Shaw, a Black SNCC activist from McComb, had been killed in Vietnam in 1965, fueling arguments against the war. Alan told us that the son in the family who had housed him in Ferriday was singled out by the local draft board because of his civil rights activity. Luther knew the time he could remain in the movement was probably limited. Our goal was to stay as long as possible.

Luther and I continued traveling door to door. Many people were still apprehensive about registering to vote. A lifetime of living with fear was not easy to overcome. A conversation with us might last five minutes, with a person eager to be pleasant but not eager to take any risk. What mattered for them was not so much what we said, but what their neighbors and family and friends did and what, if anything, happened to them if they did register.

Through Tathalia Gaston and her community we got permission to hold a second meeting at the White Plains Baptist Church. A leaflet was created on the mimeograph machine in Kosciusko and we took it with us along with the voter registration forms. The leaflet announced a civil rights meeting at the White Plains Baptist Church in McCool on Sunday, September 4.

News spread within the Black community. Every Black person who was willing to be seen at a civil rights meeting knew it was taking place. Many people stood aside and waited to see the outcome.

The white men who had shown up with guns at the first meeting also knew it was taking place. We expected them to return, but we had no way to know what they might do. We assumed Sheriff Al Malone had at least one conversation with them before the meeting, but we could not be certain of Sheriff Malone's message.

On the day of the meeting, 40 to 50 people arrived. Dock Drummond talked about the MFDP and the upcoming elections. Nash Hannah talked about organizing. Folks talked about their experiences when registering to vote, or about something that happened at their work or with a white landowner. The meeting lasted over an hour.

During that time, Gunter, Luther and I were again outside the church, walking the same wooded hillside, each of us armed. We listened for the sound of engines coming through the forest. One time a car with white men in it drove past slowly, two white faces glaring at us, but no weapons were brandished, no rifles protruded from the windows.

When the meeting ended, people cautiously filed out of the church. A few men with Nash Hannah spoke briefly with Gunter, after which two cars drove away in different directions, scouting out the road. The rest of us stood around and spoke quietly. In a few minutes the cars returned, reporting that there were no white folks waiting in ambush. People left in organized groups, while Luther and I gathered up leaflets left inside the church and locked the doors.

We had held the meeting in peace. The absence of violence was a victory.

Mr. Winfrey working with Luther Mallett and
Alan Moonves to rebuild the McCool Freedom House.
Photo by the author

Chapter 24:
No Time for Goodbye

In the early weeks of September Luther and I continued to organize in McCool. We lived in the rebuilt Freedom House, taking turns each night on guard duty. When the sun rose, breakfast was often cold instant coffee with powdered milk and hard biscuits covered with peanut butter. We got by without a kitchen. Jugs of water, soap and towels and an outhouse made the little cabin a home.

We continued to drive the area around McCool, from Ethel to the Choctaw County line. We watched every car with white men in it, waiting for any threatening move or the appearance of a gun protruding from a car window.

By this time it seemed that every Black household knew about Nash Hannah and the civil rights meetings at the White Plains Baptist Church. We continued holding meetings at Nash's house, which had more space and was more comfortable than the Freedom House. Most meeting nights Luther and I stationed ourselves on the corner of Nash's property and halted every car that started up his driveway. His home became the center of the local movement.

While Luther and I were based in McCool, the movement in Kosciusko was busy with the new "Freedom of Choice" law. It had been more than a decade since *Brown v. Board of Education* (1954), but its requirement that schools be desegregated "with all deliberate speed" had encouraged delay. The schools remained segregated in Mississippi.

The Civil Rights Act of 1964 prohibited discrimination in the public schools. It was meant to force the implementation of *Brown v. Board of Education*. Mississippi responded with a Freedom of Choice Law, which technically allowed students the freedom to pick their school, but it was passed with the intent of maintaining a dual, segregated school systems and the expectation that there would be very few Black students choosing to attend the white schools.

In the 1966-67 school year, Attala County joined Mississippi's "Freedom of Choice" plan. Implementation was to start at the high school level, which meant that students from Tipton High could sign up to attend the previously whites-only Kosciusko High.

In practice, "freedom of choice" often led to harassment and retaliation against Black students and their families. Holmes County had joined the Freedom of Choice program in 1965, and the MFDP in that county had worked very hard for a peaceful transition. The experience was not peaceful. Black students who went to the white schools were kicked and spat upon, and one parent, Mrs. Malone, was shot in the knee by a white man. The Holmes County MFDP gathered accounts of this harassment to present to the federal courts.

The Attala County MFDP threw its support behind Freedom of Choice, but it wasn't easy for a young person to decide to transfer to the white high school. Tipton High students had been using hand-me-down textbooks from the white schools during their entire education, which meant that they would start out behind white classmates in the same grade. Once a core group of Tipton students signed up for Kosciusko High, however, an effort was made to encourage more students to transfer with them.

Luther and I went to Kosciusko a few afternoons to aid this effort. Mrs. Mallett was enthusiastic and allowed both Jean and Wiley to transfer. They were joined by Sarah Robinson, Emma Ree Rayford, Shirley Yowk and Doris Yowk, who also completed the transfer forms, and by the time classes began almost 15 students took that first bold step.

Classes began on Wednesday, September 7, and almost immediately there was trouble. Wiley was taunted by some white kids in the hall, who muttered, "What are you doing here, boy?" as he walked by. Wiley turned back and gave a hard stare. This first confrontation ended without blows.

There was tension every day. White students and many of the teachers, all of whom were white, made life difficult for the Black students who had dared to enter "their" school. It took courage to show up for class each morning.[7]

At the same time, the organizing project was on the edge of change. Luther had been notified by his draft board that he had lost his student draft deferment. He was now classified 1-A and was waiting for an order to appear for a pre-induction physical exam. Betty was still gone. The school clock was ticking for Alan and me. Gunter was the only staff person planning to stay, but he also had a 90-day jail sentence hanging over him that could be imposed at any moment as well as two charges that were awaiting trial.

Luther and I continued to live in McCool. The local movement had a growing number of participants and could now be sustained on its own. We made no arrangements to leave, since just remaining was a statement, but we needed to work with Nash Hannah and others to decide the future of the McCool Freedom House. We thought there was enough time for planning.

Sunday evening, September 11, Luther stayed in McCool while I took a quick trip to Kosciusko to pick up some supplies and check with Alan about our plans. While I was at the Freedom House, the phone rang. It was Aaron Condon. He told us the police would be coming before the sun rose to arrest Alan and me on a new indictment for malicious trespass, another charge growing out of the demonstration to integrate the swimming pool at Jason Niles Park. Judge Mikell had expected us to leave when he lowered the bail over a month earlier and he had lost his patience. There was a possibility we would be taken to jail immediately to start serving the 90-day sentence imposed after our conviction for malicious mischief while awaiting trial on the new charge of malicious trespass.

Was this truly a leak of sensitive police information or was this an early warning intended to encourage our departure? Did it matter? Either way, the police would be coming for us in the morning.

Alan and I had to flee. It was a sudden and startling way to leave, but there was no reason to stay behind just to be locked up in jail. Gunter called the MFDP office in Jackson, and someone was sent to pick us up and take us to the Jackson airport. It was that quick.

I had no time to return to McCool to say goodbye to Luther. I had no time to say goodbye to the Winfreys or the Mallett family. Albert Truss and a second man went to McCool to pick up Luther and talk to Nash Hannah. While Alan packed, I brought the .38 Smith & Wesson back to the man who had sold it to me. I wasn't taking a gun with me to the airport.

I had very little to pack, since most of my stuff and my sleeping bag were in McCool. It would all be left behind. I spent a few moments sitting with Mr. and Mrs. Nash across the street, who had cared for me like family since we first arrived in January, and I needed to express my gratitude.

It was dark when a strange car arrived. I crossed the street and was greeted by the same man who had picked me up in June at the Jackson airport, when I had arrived looking for a friendly face. Alan and I threw our gear in his trunk and said goodbye to Gunter. At the man's instructions we lay down on the floor in the back of his car.

One block from the Freedom House a pair of headlights from a car suddenly appeared behind us and illuminated the inside of the car. "Just stay down," the driver instructed us. Alan and I pressed ourselves harder against the floor mats. The headlights then blinked twice and the car kept a steady pace behind us. We had an escort.

After a few blocks we took a sharp left and entered the darkness of the Natchez Trace. Alan and I finally sat up, peering carefully out the car windows. We were both in a daze. The forest was dark under a star-filled sky, an occasional electric light from a farmhouse shining in the distance. All was silent except for the hum of the car's engine.

In less than an hour we were dropped off at the Jackson airport. Someone at the MFDP had made reservations for us, and we went to the counter and paid for tickets to Atlanta. I watched for anyone in a police uniform, but no one approached us. We boarded a plane in the darkness and landed in Atlanta as the sun was rising.

We could have traveled on, but we needed some time to decompress, so we took a bus to the downtown area. I felt as though I had been lifted by a time machine out of rural Mississippi. Atlanta was bustling with the morning commute, and soon Alan and I sat together at an integrated restaurant counter having breakfast and a few cups of coffee.

Restless and wired, we walked the city for hours. I felt jumpy. I remained alert for any threat, but no one paid us any attention. When lunchtime came in the afternoon we found a Black-run barbeque and just hung out in a booth eating, drinking beer and listening to Motown.

"Look around, Matt," Alan said pensively. "We may never be so welcomed in this setting again." As we talked it out, he meant we might never again be accepted so casually in the Black community. We had one last beer.

Somehow we found the bus to the airport. Alan flew back to school in Boston and I took a flight to New York. My parents picked me up at the airport. They were relieved and very happy to see me. When we got home, I had another beer.

In the days that followed I visited David Saft in Greenwich Village and talked and talked and drank cheap red wine. We talked about fear. David had worked in a SNCC-sponsored project in Maryland, the Cambridge Nonviolent Action Committee, and had experienced the threat of violence firsthand.

I borrowed the family car and drove to Baltimore to visit Wendy. Driving the speed of Highway 95 for hours was mesmerizing, and I took the exit without slowing down. I hit the brakes when I approached an intersection and a stop sign, but I lost traction, the car started spinning and I slammed into a metal guard rail. Somehow I was able to drive away. I spent the night at her family home as Wendy calmed me down.

Back in Valley Stream, I retreated to the basement and wrote down some memories about Mississippi. I gathered up leaflets, letters, notes, even our Freedom Now bumper sticker. There were also a few photographs, but my box camera was still in McCool with a roll of film in it. I stashed everything in a box and left it behind at my parents' house.

I returned to Oberlin. I was conflicted about being in school, despite the risk of being drafted. I was restless and disconnected from classes. Veterans of the movement, people like Dick Klausner and Joe Gross, understood what I was feeling and encouraged me to stay. Wendy encouraged me to stay. My good friend, Bill Ewell, sat with me and asked, "So how has the experience in Mississippi changed you?" I didn't know yet.

How could I leave these people? I stayed.

I called Gunter regularly from the pay phone in the dormitory. He told me Luther had also fled Kosciusko in the middle of the night to avoid lengthy jail time. Someone from the MFDP had taken him to Arizona. Gunter said he was tried on the charges from the meeting in McCool and had been convicted on the charge of pointing and aiming a deadly weapon. The judge had sentenced him to six months in prison. He was out on appeal and would mail me my stuff from McCool if I sent him some money. I mailed him a check.

Luther had indeed fled to Arizona. He had been taken out of Mississippi on a motorcycle by MFDP organizer Ronald Fox and dropped off in Arizona, where he got a factory job. He ignored an order to appear for a pre-induction physical. Within a few weeks he was arrested and given the choice of enlisting or going to jail. He enlisted in the Navy. My parents sent me a letter Luther mailed to Valley Stream.

> Dear Matt,
> The day you left town, it took something away from me. We had worked together, slept together, rode together, just about every thing we did it together. That's what made me feel so close to you like we were brothers. Often I wish we were still together. People in this mean world would only stop and think, things would be a hell lot better.
> Your friend,
> Luther

I called Gunter again. He hadn't had time to send my stuff. I continued to call. He was busy, he was busy, and then he was gone. The phone to the Freedom House was disconnected. I called Mrs. Nash, who was glad to hear from me and glad to know I was well. She told me that Gunter had fled because they were about to send him to jail. Yes, she and Mr. Nash were fine. I wrote to some of the high school activists who had given me an address and who might know what happened to Gunter. I got a letter at Oberlin from Shirley Yowk:

> Dear Matt,
> I was very glad to hear from you. I had given up on you writing and was very surprised to come home from school and found you had written. I hope you understand that you have lied to me because you promised me that you would write in two and half weeks but I suppose you were busy and I will forgive you this time. It is true that Gunter has left Miss.
> Jean has probably told you that she likes Kosciusko High School. Well! I don't like it, I hate it. I probably won't make my grade this year but I'm not going back up there next year.

If you see Tim or Alan tell them I said hello and everything
is going rough. (smile).

Take care of yourself and don't do anything I won't do.

Love,

Shirley

A

N

SOON - Shirley

W

E

R

I imagined returning to Kosciusko and wrote to the Lawyers'
Committee for Civil Rights to find out if there was any way I could return
safely. The response I got was clear:

Dear Matt,

I have your letter of November 11th. Upon its receipt, I
reread my earlier letter to you and rechecked the files. You could
return to Mississippi, but would be subject to arrest and trial.

If some questions remain unanswered, please ask further.

Sincerely yours,

Denison Ray

The group of us who had been full-time organizers in Kosciusko for
the MFDP had been scattered. What was the result of our efforts? The
final word from Mississippi that year came from Jean Mallett, in a letter
Jean sent on behalf of herself and Wiley on December 6, 1966:

Dear Matt,

I received your letter and was very glad to hear from you.

We are doing O.K. in school, I couldn't say fine because
some of us aren't doing so well.

Gunther left for California and was going by way of Arizona
and see Luther. I don't suppose that Gunther got to see Luther
because Luther has now reported for duty in the Navy on the

30th of November.

Things are quiet around here but the project is still on the move, and I don't think it will ever die. I am sort of proud of my town. Wiley or I either would never mind giving you a general rundown of things.

Wiley started to write, but I hope you don't mind me writing.

My mother sends her love. You know she thought you were a pretty level person.

Thanks for letting us hear about Tim and Alan they were some nice kids or young men also. I still feel sort of guilty about Tim's accident while he was down here working for us.

If you see them again tell them we are still yelling for them.

You take care and tell Alan and Tim also.

I'll see you in Freedom Land.

Jean

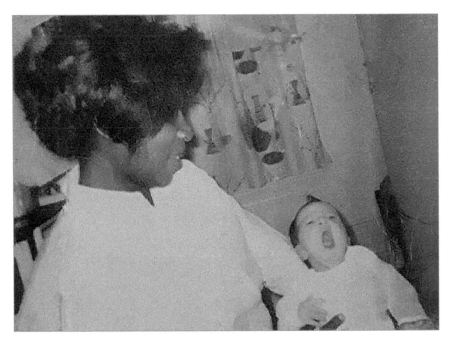

Betty Jones with daughter Consuela Frentz.
Photo courtesy of grandson Lawrence Robinson.

Fire at the Freedom House

Epilogue

1.

In 1969 I graduated from Oberlin and was passed over by the draft board. Swept up in the whirlwind of the late sixties, my life merged with the chaos of the antiwar movement, romantic relationships and life in collectives and communes. All I knew from letters was that Luther was in the Navy and that Wiley had been drafted and sent to Vietnam. I had no idea what had happened to Betty and Gunter or to any of the activists living in Attala County.

Mississippi continued to haunt my dreams. Kosciusko pulled on my heart and my memories. In 1973, mindful that I could be arrested and jailed if I returned, I called Kosciusko and spoke to the new city attorney, Chatwin Jackson.

I explained my situation and told him I wanted to visit. Mr. Jackson listened patiently as I described my legal situation. I asked directly if I still faced arrest if I returned to Attala County.

"Well," he said, "Y'all come back, and we'll find out."

I stayed away.

2.

In 1978 I was living in Oakland, California. I had worked for years in a warehouse and was active in an insurgent movement called TDU, Teamsters for A Democratic Union.

Alan Moonves came to visit. He was unemployed and chain-smoking. We drove to Mendocino County and stayed at a commune started by Oberlin students. He helped me fix a window on a small cabin I had built with friends.

Alan had come to California for a job interview but failed to get the job. He returned to New York City. Two weeks later he committed suicide.

I will miss him forever.

3.

In 1980 I entered law school in San Francisco. Through a combination of good luck and hard work, I did well. I joined the National Lawyers Guild, an organization of progressive attorneys. A month after taking the bar exam I met my wife, Shelly Fox. We got married in 1984 and started a family in 1985.

At age 42 there was every reason to be fully satisfied with life. But, at night, my dream world was still filled with fitful memories of being chased through the back roads and pine forests of Mississippi.

4.

In 2004, I attended the National Lawyers Guild annual convention in Birmingham, Alabama. John Lewis was the keynote speaker. Could I cross the state line and visit Mississippi?

Slow to the internet, I learned from my wife that online I could scroll through phone listings looking for Luther. There were now 26 listings for Malletts in the Kosciusko phone book. I worked my way through the list and made many calls before I finally reached the number for Mallett, L. J.

"Hello," I said. "Is Luther Mallet there?"

"You mean the Luther Mallett who was involved in the civil rights movement?" responded a female voice I did not recognize.

"Yes ma'am, I do."

"Luther!" the voice called out. "It's Matt on the phone."

Luther and I talked for an hour. It had been Jean who had answered the phone. "L.J. Mallett" in the phone listing was their mother, Lenora J. Mallett. Luther told me that during the war in Vietnam he had been stationed on an aircraft carrier in the Pacific. He now lived in Southern California with his family, including a grandchild. Wiley had been boots on the ground during the war, but had safely returned to Kosciusko. They both had suffered from the trauma.

Jean had stayed in Kosciusko and had become an elementary school teacher in the small town of Sallis in Attala County. Wiley lived down the road with his family. Many of their friends had moved out of the state after the sixties, though Shirley Adams and others were still in Mississippi. Luther had heard that Betty had died of cancer, but he knew nothing about Gunter.

One surprise was that a granddaughter of Elmore and Beatrice Winfrey was now a famous personality, the incomparable Oprah Winfrey.

Luther gave me the sad news that he and Jean and Wiley were gathered at the old family home in Kosciusko because their mother was in a coma, on a hospital bed in the living room. There was no way to know how much longer she would be alive. Luther was back in Mississippi to be a caregiver. I was determined to visit.

This time I called the Mayor of Kosciusko, Jimmy Cockroft. He did not recognize my name. I told him I had been a civil rights worker in the county back in 1966 and wanted to return to visit some old friends. Were there still warrants out for my arrest?

"Well, who is it you want to visit?" he asked.

"Luther Mallett and the Mallett family. And the folks who put me up, if they're still alive." I replied.

"Who might that be?" he asked.

"Elmore and Beatrice Winfrey," I replied.

"Give me your number," he said. "I'll check things out and call you tomorrow."

Mayor Cockroft called back the next day.

"We didn't find any outstanding warrants for you," he said. "We'd love to have you come back and experience some of our Southern hospitality."

My old friend Wendy agreed to join me for a road trip in the Deep South. She had spent time in Alabama after Oberlin and had fond memories of Southern food. She flew into Birmingham and met me at the National Lawyers Guild convention. We headed south in Alabama until we reached the Mississippi border east of Meridian. There was the familiar Welcome to Mississippi billboard and the same state flag, in 2004 still flaunting the battle flag of the Confederacy in the upper left quadrant. I felt a ripple of fear.

We drove for a few miles until we pulled off at a roadside café and settled in for a meal. I sat with my back exposed to the door while we studied the menu. Wendy was looking forward to eggs and biscuits as I began to fidget in my seat. Suddenly I stood up and looked around the restaurant.

I couldn't sit near the door. I had to change seats and have my back to the wall, so I could keep an eye on the restaurant and anyone who might come through the door. The waitress was surprised, but she took our orders. Wendy, who had been a therapist for years, was not surprised.

"You might have a touch of PTSD there, Matt" she suggested. "There's really nothing to fear."

After eating we drove from Meridian through Neshoba County on Highway 19, past Rock Cut Road, where Chaney, Goodman and Schwerner were murdered in 1964, driving the same road they had taken. There was a growing tightness in my shoulders. I had to get out of the car and walk around. We stopped at the courthouse square in Philadelphia. The sidewalks were cracked and many of the storefronts needed repair, but the courthouse itself looked just as sharp as when we marched there in 1966.

A white man stood behind two large kettles on the street corner selling boiled salted peanuts. We bought a large bag and drove on to Kosciusko.

5.

"Luther? Is that really you?" I was incredulous.

The man greeting me looked nothing like the Luther Mallett of 1966. My visual image, reinforced by years of looking at old photos, was of a slender, jaunty companion. There was now a portly man with a huge smile filling the door frame.

"Matt! It's great to see you! Hey, there may be a lot more Luther than there used to be, but there's a lot less hair on that head of yours. I'd still recognize you anywhere."

We laughed and embraced.

Soon we were driving through town in his truck to get fresh food. We headed to one of the Sunflower Markets. Walking down the aisle, Luther started kidding around with a young white woman. I had an immediate sense of alarm.

"Luther!" I said. "I don't think we want to be attracting attention."

"Matt," he said, with a touch of surprise. "There's nobody looking for us, and people mix everywhere. If you really want to keep watch, look for some old guy from back in the day. But," Luther added with a chuckle, "he probably won't recognize us."

We drove with Wendy to the Mallett farm, where his mother lay on a hospital bed in the living room. I've been told that sometimes one can speak to a person in a coma and be understood. I took the opportunity to lean over and speak with Mrs. Mallett for a few minutes, thanking her for her warmth and bravery and strength.

Jean was living in the house while she and Wiley and Luther cared for their mother. Luther did the cooking and served platters of ribs and greens as we sat in the kitchen and revisited old times.

The next day we drove around Kosciusko. Elmore and Beatrice Winfrey had passed away as had Pearl and Edgar Nash. The Freedom House was gone, just dirt and grass. A new brick house sat on the corner hill, which no longer looked steep at all, and another brick house sat next door. Everywhere people were open and friendly.

We drove to McCool.

The old brick buildings run by the Bowie brothers still stood, but they were abandoned. We went looking for Nash Hannah. He had died years earlier. We met one of his great-granddaughters. Luther and I wrote her a note extolling Nash, writing "Black and white together" with our names

I had another surge of fear as we took the dirt road toward the old McCool Freedom House. It was gone, nothing there now but a patch of ground. Through the trees one could now see a much-enlarged brick church.

People who lived down the road came by and visited. One Black woman said she had been seven years old when we rebuilt the Freedom House, and she remembered a gun battle that caused her to duck below the window. "I was scared," she said. "But that was a long time ago."

I asked her father how people got along in the county these days.

"Blacks and whites here," he said, "gets along now like bees and honey."

6.

Lenora Mallett passed away within two weeks of my visit. I flew back to Kosciusko, too late for her funeral. I drove to the cemetery and laid flowers on her grave.

On the same visit I was introduced to a white man named Preston Hughes. He candidly talked about growing up in Kosciusko.

As a young man he had been a firm believer that when Goodman, Chaney and Schwerner went missing, it was really a hoax, that they were up in New York laughing at white people in Mississippi. He believed it because his elders and his senators told him it was a hoax. When the bodies of the civil rights workers were found buried in an earthen dam in Neshoba County, his thinking was changed forever.

Preston Hughes was now part of a dinner club building racial unity in Attala County.

7.

In 2005 I posted a short statement on a website for veterans of the civil rights movement, crmvet.org. In December I got an e-mail which identified the sender as Love Tours.

The e-mail was from Gunter Frentz. He said a reporter had brought my posting to his attention. He gave me his phone number.

I called. It was Gunter on the other end. We had a disjointed conversation. We talked about the piece I had written on the civil rights website. He said he had been living in New Orleans but had been driven out by Hurricane Katrina and moved to Fort Worth, Texas.

We want our stories to end in a certain way. We want clarity, moral redemption, some uplifting closure. Instead, what I learned repulsed me. Love Tours had morphed into something described as pleasure tours. Gunter was taking men, and possibly some women, on sex tours to Thailand.

A numbing coldness spread from my feet to my heart. I tried to talk with Gunter about what he was doing, but the conversation went nowhere. He justified his business as willing customers engaged in legal activities. I saw it as part of human trafficking.

We never spoke again.

8.

My website posting brought an e-mail from a production company in New York. Had I really been housed by the Winfreys? When they learned the whole story and saw the photographs of Mr. Winfrey directing the rebuilding of the Freedom House in McCool, they flew me to Mississippi.

Luther and I were featured on the PBS special titled "Oprah's Roots."

9.

I got an e-mail from a white man.

I came across your posting regarding your civil rights work in my hometown of Kosciusko, Mississippi.

I am ashamed to admit that I was one of those nasty white kids who gave the African-American kids (especially Emma Ree Rayford and the Malletts) a hard time when they attended the formerly white high school. I have often thought that I would like to apologize to them and thank them for helping bring some badly needed change to Kosciusko. They truly were unbelievably brave and strong.

You helped free us all.

Ralph Jennings.

10.

I was contacted by a young man from Vicksburg named Lawrence Robinson, who found me through the same crmvet.org website.

He told me that he was a grandson of Betty Jones and Gunter Frentz. They had a child, Consuela Frentz, who had three sons, Lawrence and his two brothers. Betty and Gunter did not stay together. He told me that his grandmother, Betty, had died of cancer in the 1980's, the same sad news that had reached Luther. Over time Lawrence sent me photographs, including one of Betty with her daughter which is included in this book.

Lawrence Robinson reached out because he wanted to learn more about what his grandparents had done during the civil rights movement. I was able to send him much of the material that appears in this book and confirm that his grandparents had been an inspiration in Attala County.

11.

Writing this memoir, I contacted the Attala County Library and was put in contact with the genealogy librarian, Ann Breedlove. By e-mail, I expressed interest in *The Star- Herald* articles on many topics, including the Freedom of Choice school plan of 1966. Ms. Breedlove, who was very helpful, wrote back, "Although some things changed in 1966, I don't remember going to school with any Black people until about 1968."

I told her I was really certain about 1966, and mentioned Shirley Yowk. Ms. Breedlove then remembered that she had been in school with

Shirley and her sister Doris Yowk, who worked at a bank on the court-house square. I called Doris Yowk, who did not remember my name. She took my phone number and agreed to pass it on to her sister.

The phone rang.

"Matt!" It was Shirley Yowk, calling from Missouri. "You know you never answered my letter. I can't believe you're getting in touch now!" We talked for over an hour. She said that just two weeks earlier she had spoken at her church about going to the white high school, about being spat upon and shunned. She remembered the marches and picketing and the arrests at Jason Niles Park. We remembered some details differently, but whether it was a city bus or a school bus which carried the students to jail, to jail they went.

After I left Kosciusko, a cross was burned on the lawn in front of the Yowk family home. Shirley told me she watched from a window as white men set the cross ablaze. "Sometimes I can't believe what we endured in those days," she said. She left Mississippi as soon as she graduated from high school.

12.

A month later Shirley Yowk called me back.

"Matt," she asked with urgency, "have you heard what happened to Michael Brown? He was an unarmed Black teenager shot to death by a white policeman."

The town she had moved to in Missouri was Ferguson.

The killing of Michael Brown sparked a movement. That movement was named Black Lives Matter.

Fire at the Freedom House

Notes

1   Sally Belfrage. *Freedom Summer* (New York: The Viking Press, 1968), 10.

2   Elizabeth Sutherland Martinez, ed. *Letters from Mississippi* (Brookline: Zephyr Press, 2002), 100.

3   Richard Roisman, "Notes from Mississippi." *The Oberlin Review*, Vol. 94, no. 29 (February 11, 1966), 5.

4   This quote is from the FBI files. It was obtained from the National Archives pursuant to a request under the Freedom of Information Act.

5   Stokely Carmichael. *Ready for Revolution* (Scribner's, 2003), 505. A history of the Meredith March can be found in the work of Aram Goudsousian, *Down to the Crossroads*, (Farrar, Straus and Giroux, 2014).

6   Stokely Carmichael. *Ready for Revolution* (Scribner's, 2003), 379.

7   The harassment that accompanied "Freedom of Choice" in many Mississippi counties led to the U.S. Supreme Court ruling in Alexander v. Holmes County Board of Education (1969) 396 U.S. 19, which ordered the immediate end to segregation in public schools. Attala County complied and merged the segregated schools into one integrated public school system. White Attala County residents lacked the resources or motivation to establish private segregated schools, and public education in Attala County has been integrated ever since that time.

Acknowledgements

I started writing this memoir when I first returned from Mississippi, but I couldn't do it. The best I could manage was to make a list of names associated with Kosciusko, Ethel and McCool. I put these pages in a box with photographs, leaflets, letters, notes from conversations and a random collection of papers. The box sat at my parents' house for years.

When I first started writing this memoir with the serious intention of completing it, I had a recurrence of a nightmare which had lived in my dream world for years. I'm a passenger in a car at night on a dirt road in Mississippi. We are being chased by a vehicle which is gaining on us. We jump from the car and start running through the woods. A shot rings out. They are gaining on us. I wake up screaming.

Fortunately for me, my spouse, Shelly Fox, shook my arm and said, "You're okay. You're okay. You're safe at home and everything is fine." Shelly put up with the nightmare and more than a decade of watching me struggle with a keyboard and the computer. I am deeply grateful.

They say that writing is a lonely pursuit, but I could not have written this book alone. A friend directed me to Jane Staw, an author and writing coach. She worked with me for years in a small cottage which she considered a writing room but where I sometimes found a form of memoir therapy. She helped me get through a first full draft.

Ani Tascian and the other students in her writing class, which I took for over a year, provided important and supportive critical feedback.

Many people encouraged me. Luther Mallett sat and talked with me for hours. Once I called him to talk about the events described in the book which took place in a large tent. "Luther," I said to him, "how can I put that in? I won't believe it myself if I read it in someone else's book." "Matt," he replied, "you got to put it in. That's what happened." I have tried to follow that advice throughout this memoir.

Jean Mallett and Wiley Mallett sat for long interviews and encouraged me. Preston Hughes and Katherine Carr Esters shared their stories of living in Kosciusko. Steve Early read the manuscript and gave me important feedback. Phil Hutchings helped me think about the use of language. My friend Wendy Forbush read the book and gave me a sense of purpose. Marie Wilson read the book and gave me critical feedback, even when I called multiple times for help. Alice Lawrence was incredibly patient as I struggled to learn from her computer skills which for many others are quite basic. Joe Gross, David Saft, Ilene Abrams, Alan Miller and Joe Berkson all helped. My friend Jane Margolis told me multiple times to "keep writing!" and read the entire last draft of the manuscript. I am so very thankful.

Design credit goes to Dave Chapple, who brought skill, patience and talent to the final creation of this book.

Of course, any mistakes in the manuscript are my responsibility. Sometimes I made new mistakes when I corrected old ones.

Finally, I am forever thankful to the people in the Black community of Attala County and individuals throughout Mississippi who welcomed me into their homes and into their lives, who allowed me to join in their struggles, who risked everything and who inspired me to always believe that we can build a better world.

CPSIA information can be obtained
at www.ICGtesting.com
Printed in the USA
BVHW060251110821
614046BV00005B/56